PRAISE FOR *LONG YARN SHORT*

'Brilliant exposé of the toxic debacle that is family policing. Essential reading. If you think the state can be a safe parent, read this book.' **Melissa Lucashenko**

'Vanessa speaks to the child in us all: vulnerable, loving and in need of being loved. Read this and remember that a better tomorrow starts with our children.' **Stan Grant**

'This is a song of defiance and fierce hope that demands to be heard. You will not forget the unconquerable spirit that animates this story. Out of injustice and loss, Vanessa crafts a vision of a better future based on connection to culture and community. In this extraordinary book, she weaves her life into the broader fabric of Australia's genocidal history and challenges the reader to join her in the uplift of First Nations children and families.' **Professor Michael Salter**

'*Long Yarn Short* needs to be on the shelf of every Australian living on unceded land and beyond. With precision and courage, Vanessa Turnbull-Roberts lacerates the colonialist institutions that white Australia still hides behind to degrade and harm First Nations people. A testimony of survival and the indefatigable pride of Aboriginal communities, *Long Yarn Short* is an essential text from an unstoppable force.' **Clementine Ford**

T0356610

'*Long Yarn Short* is a must-read, powerful, first-hand account of survival in the out-of-home care system. Turnbull-Roberts is fierce and unflinching as she seeks to hold the system to account but never loses her warmth, heart and strong senses of self and community. This book is a must-read for anyone wanting to better understand why the numbers of First Nations children in out-of-home care continue to rise – and what needs to be done to change it – by someone who has been through it and continues to fight for reform.'
Distinguished Professor Larissa Behrendt

'A deeply moving first-hand account by a survivor of child removal. Defying great odds, Turnbull-Roberts overcame the insurmountable obstacles put in her way, and her strength and tenacity proved to be her saving grace. We have heard the stories from the Stolen Generations, but this book is quite unique in its particular narrative of presence and place. One can acknowledge the history of forced removals, but we can never identify with the lived experience of those who tell it and write it from their own perspectives. For this is her personal story, one which will add to the ever-growing truth-telling accounts by First Nations peoples that are so needed in these times.'
Dr Jackie Huggins

'Vanessa Turnbull-Roberts has written a profound and compelling tale of surviving the family policing system. *Long Yarn Short* is an honest, searing account of being removed from one's family, and the system's impact on a child and the community around them. Vanessa speaks directly to readers with a firm power and clear-eyed hope, calling for the abolition of the family policing system and the complete reimagination of how we support the most vulnerable in society, guided by the millennia of First Nations folks who have come before. This book is a true gift.' **Yassmin Abdel-Magied**

'With the passion and insight of a survivor, Vanessa Turnbull-Roberts unmasks the Australian family policing system's pretence of saving children to expose its colonial design and portray its harm to Aboriginal families. *Long Yarn Short* is not only a compelling yarn of state-inflicted trauma but also a powerful call for abolition and community-based, restorative support. Recommended reading for anyone working toward a safer and more caring world.' **Professor Dorothy Roberts**

Vanessa Turnbull-Roberts is a proud Bundjalung Widubul-Wiabul woman, who holds degrees in both law and social work, and was recognised with an Australian Human Rights Medal in 2019. She is a human rights lawyer and Fulbright scholar whose current research is focused on unveiling the intersections of human rights, child removal and the implications of forcible removal, ensuring that First Nations child survivors and those impacted are heard, while providing solutions towards ending child removal. In 2024 Vanessa was appointed the inaugural Aboriginal and Torres Strait Islander Children and Young People Commissioner for the Australian Capital Territory.

VANESSA TURNBULL-ROBERTS

LONG YARN SHORT

WE ARE STILL HERE

First published 2024 by University of Queensland Press
PO Box 6042, St Lucia, Queensland 4067 Australia

The University of Queensland Press (UQP) acknowledges the Traditional Owners and
their custodianship of the lands on which UQP operates. We pay our respects to their
Ancestors and their descendants, who continue cultural and spiritual connections to
Country. We recognise their valuable contributions to Australian and global society.

uqp.com.au
reception@uqp.com.au

Copyright © Vanessa Turnbull-Roberts 2024
The moral rights of the author have been asserted.

This book is copyright. Except for private study, research, criticism or reviews,
as permitted under the Copyright Act, no part of this book may be reproduced,
stored in a retrieval system, or transmitted in any form or by any means without
prior written permission. Enquiries should be made to the publisher.

Cover design by Jenna Lee
Cover photographs courtesy of the author
Typeset in 12.5/17.5 pt Bembo Std by Post Pre-press Group, Brisbane
Printed in Australia by McPherson's Printing Group

University of Queensland Press is assisted by the Australian Government through
Creative Australia, its principal arts investment and advisory body.

A catalogue record for this book is available from the National Library of Australia

ISBN 978 0 7022 6868 7 (pbk)
ISBN 978 0 7022 7000 0 (epdf)
ISBN 978 0 7022 7001 7 (epub)

University of Queensland Press uses papers that are natural, renewable and recyclable
products made from wood grown in well-managed forests and other controlled sources.
The logging and manufacturing processes conform to the environmental regulations of
the country of origin.

Aboriginal and Torres Strait Islander readers are respectfully cautioned that this
publication contains images/mentions of people who have passed away.

*For the children and ancestors who didn't
get to come home and for those yet to come home.
We won't stop fighting for your rightful place of return.*

To Mum and Dad:
I am sorry for the pain these systems put on you.
I hope you know I see your smiles, eyes, personality and love
in your granddaughter. Every mark and bloodline within her
are a connection to the ancestors, to the power of who we are.
You deserve to be here, to see it all, to have the joy.
For that, I won't stop demanding more.

Solutions to reimagine a better world combating family policing.
For you, for me, for us.

We move together.

CONTENTS

AUTHOR'S NOTE

I AM NOT NAIVE TO THE problems that exist in this place, but what I ask of you, as a reader, is to take into consideration what had to have happened for it to get so bad. Things must have happened.

My parents are my world, and I wish they were here to see the person I am today. I write this book as a gift to the world to make it better. To remember there are better solutions and paths to take. My nan also kept me protected, all through my childhood years through to adulting. Spirit. You'll learn about this in my long yarn short. My people, my culture, are the reason I have survived.

We don't need to add harm. In fact, there's a whole new reality we can create.

I was the kid scared.

I was the kid surviving.

I did not need to get stolen.

My community needed help. Not the pathologising type, the real type, where the harm leaves and the community is strengthened. There were so many other options than taking us kids away and separating families.

I am moved to offer you this long yarn short, simply because I am finally at a time in my life when I am prepared to share a bit more with the world. I believe there can be special things that come from truthful offerings, for change and the better.

I want to thank all those who believe in this work, this change and this story, who believe that we can create a better world and ensure that no-one gets left behind. *Long Yarn Short* was birthed out of a willingness to call out Australia's family policing system, one that does not operate on the foundations of love, community and care. Sadly, as Indigenous people, we know this story too well.

As both a survivor and the author of this book, I take joy in sharing this long yarn short with you.

Thank you to my family, my community, my ancestors and my daughter, Waitui.

This is for our children and young people. This is for a better tomorrow.

I wish you well on this yarn.

THIS IS

MY YARN

IMAGINE YOU ARE JUST TEN-AND-A-HALF years old, growing up in your community, connected deeply to your cultural ties, family.

You live in social housing. You know you are a little bit different to the rest of the privileged world, but you are rich. You are rich in the love of your parents, the food that you eat.

You are broke, yes, but the plate is there, and the stomach is nourished. At times your clothes are a bit dirty, and yeah there are circumstances where you should have been safer.

But instead of the state providing the support and love to a family, a community or kin, you are stolen in the middle of the night by police officers and a 'case worker'. They come up the stairs to your second-floor housing apartment ... your home.

Just before closing your eyes, you hear your father say, 'Big girl ... I am so sorry, pack some things, they are coming.' He says it in a way that is all too familiar. They are not even at the door yet, but your dad knows, the power of the gut feeling – or in your case, in your cultural ways, you know something bad is on the way when you see the willie wag, which is a messenger bird. This is the old people letting you know something bad is about to happen ... Except in this moment, it's not the willie wag late at night; it's the red and blue lights flashing, the sirens wailing, coming down your street.

You are just a kid. Your stomach immediately knows. You have no choice in this moment but to survive.

ACKNOWLEDGEMENT

WOULD LIKE TO ACKNOWLEDGE THE stories, journeys, strengths, healing and love of my people, who have continued to practice deep acts of love, care and justice. They are our past, our future and importantly our present – physically and spiritually. They are the raw and true definition of what it means to stand strong, to demand love and to demand justice. These people, my people, are the children who continue to be silenced, and the people who never got to come home. I want to acknowledge you.

I wrote the majority of this book on the lands of the Gadigal, Bidjigal and Wurrang people, and the rest on the lands of the Lenni-Lenape people in the United States. I also acknowledge that my story is one that holds similar collective pain and injustices, is connected to the violence of this nation, which has been written across many sacred countries of these lands.

When I was stolen, I was ripped from one country and taken to another. I believe that the ancestors of my Bundjalung Widubul–Wiabul people stayed with me, and they saved me.

I remember the dark, scary nights. I remember going from strange place to strange place, scared every night in some of the foster placements I was put in. I was terrified. I remember feeling so scared.

As you read through this book, I ask gently that you take the time to honour the country you are on. I challenge you to think about the story that may have taken place on that land. It is likely a story of survival, a story of lifestyle and nature, a story of strength, but also a story of violence and harm.

These stories all hold a sacred meaning to place, connection and community. They also hold a place in understanding the implications of colonisation and understanding where, why and how this plays a role in today's society.

If there is one thing I can promise you, it is this: there is still blood on the land and in the waters, blood from the violence and the pain that still ripples through. Where you may now see buildings, corporations and concrete jungles, there were once villages, nation groups, kinship systems and song lines of the lands. Where you see homeless people laying in the street, there were once trees, nature and community all around.

Whether you are overseas reading this book or here in Australia, I challenge you to learn the story of the land you are on. As Indigenous people, our lands continue to be under attack across the world. No matter where you are situated, the land and history of our people is interconnected deeply. This is who we are. Our transnational solidarity, our struggle and our strength are our greatest connection.

The land is me, and I am the land. Have you ever taken time when you are just sitting? To look at the trees? Often you will see two big trees, and then a few more behind, and others extended around. This is our kinship system in the land, our connection to all things around us. Those two front trees represent the parents, the ones around represent the children, cousins, siblings – aunties, uncles, guncles. When you see the land, try to imagine a whole family, a whole community.

Our survival is because of the land, and we will continue to survive.

So, who am I?

I am angry. I am hurt. I am proud. I am strong. I was stolen. I exist in multitudes, but I want you to remember that I was stolen. My parents did not give consent and, even when the court processes began, there was coercion of state force – 'it's in her best interests' – to the point where my dad did not want to see the impact the systems were having.

I want you to walk along this journey, as a reader, remembering that the author of this work has lived the injustices of the family policing system here in Australia.

I want you to imagine being ten-and-a-half years old. I want you to imagine being tucked up in bed, about to close your eyes and then suddenly feeling this fear, this anxiety, this energy entering the surroundings of your home. I want you to imagine your dad going onto the balcony, terrified, knowing what is about to happen. I want you to hear him yelling, 'Bub ... Big girl. I am so sorry, but they are coming to get you.'

I was just a kid.

I was just about to close my eyes.

When I was stolen, I was ripped from one country and taken to another, from my family to strangers. This is what the family policing system does. It separates families and rips newborns away from their parents. It takes a child from one world and places it in another. But we don't think about this.

We think that the removal of children must occur because of severe danger – or what the family policing system feels is danger in their eyes. Racism lies at the foundation of this practice. And to this day, the system continues to hurt our people. Our children, our fathers, our mothers, our aunties, our uncles, our grandmothers and our grandfathers. There is a strange deep addiction to the removal of Black children, one where it is often non-Indigenous tools of the state just so deeply addicted to contributing to the harm of our families, instead of offering support.

ACKNOWLEDGEMENT

The family policing system is alive, and yet help is not on the way when you reach out to the departmental services here in Australia. What I continue to see is people, who are simply subject to poverty and often survivors themselves of family policing, reach out for support and have their own children ripped apart from them. Imagine that: asking for help and being punished.

In fact, I hope through the stories and the knowledge I pass on that by the end of this book you will agree with me. Because, together, we can truly look beyond the family policing regime and instead rebuild our families and communities. We can look to transformative justice and build worlds of practice, of community, love and belonging.

Children are often taken away on grounds of neglect where there isn't any evidence of severe abuse. And often a person's definition of neglect depends on their personal perspectives and experience – meaning it's different to what another may constitute as neglect. This form of state intervention and family separation is a common experience for First Nations families here in Australia.

I have seen newborns taken from their families, simply because their mother and parent responds to state intervention with rage. The state then uses this against the mother, and reports *mother's use of anger*, arguing that the child is therefore neglected. Never once considering that, maybe, the mother just does not want state intervention. Or that the child protection services are in fact doing the harm – that they are the neglectful ones.

This is deeply rooted in racism and a denial of the emotion that every Aboriginal person has the right to feel when history is being repeated. This very response is a reminder that Aboriginal women simply do not get to be angry, have rage, feel hurt and be triggered by the violence of the family policing system.

Before we go any further, also know this: I am a proud Bundjalung Widubul-Wiabul woman.

Identifying this is crucial to claiming my identity and ensuring that no matter what space I am situated in, whether that is in storytelling, activism or legal work, that I am firmly rooted in the ground of my place, where I come from and where I am going when I transform from physical living to the dreaming of my people. This is where I come from, this is fundamentally who I am.

As traditional custodians of these lands, we identify through our cultural language groups and kinship systems of being. This is something not really known to many non-Indigenous people. The idea of living together in kin, that our parents are beyond mum and dad, and the roles of aunty and uncle add kinship to our sovereignty and being – this plays an important role of guidance and healing for our connection. It's how we have sustained our existence of community and support, being able to know that we all have different roles.

So, as a child being taken from my community and way of life and forced into homes where my culture was not respected or liberated was extremely hard. I was worlds apart from everything I had ever known. But my world and culture never left my heart or my fight.

The reality is, they stole me too late.

But if I am honest, even when younger children are taken, we know that our children, long-term, always want to come home, to return.

I am a survivor of the family policing system, a system that actively promotes, targets and harms First Nations people.

These policing systems started with protectionist and paternalistic policies and practices with the targeting of our elders, generations back.

Under the Stolen Generations regimes of racially charged legislation, First Nations people were forcibly removed from their country and families to be taught and 're-educated'. First Nations children were identified at institutions and local community family areas, such as hospitals and other spaces, and then social workers, doctors, governments, churches and welfare bodies forcibly removed many Aboriginal and Torres Strait Islander children from their families. The decision-makers were those people in power.

Children were just on country, in their homes, their communities – still taken.

Children were existing, loving, thriving – still taken.

Children were on their mother's breast – still taken.

Children were out walking, hunting – still taken.

Children were Indigenous children – still taken.

As has been documented extensively in the *Bringing Them Home* report, First Nations people were also subject to prohibitions against speaking traditional language and ultimately treated as second-class citizens subject to physical, psychological and sexual abuse.

The conduct of these removals was the foundation of superiority and inferiority, implying that my people are lower than those who are white. The superior class of people had the free will to access, harm and violate our bodies, communities and country. This was a genuine standpoint, inflicted in both policies and the law to do this to my people. To this day there has never been the opportunity to heal, and if I am honest, I do not think there will be healing. You touch our children, you hurt our people, you break our communities, harm our countries – that pain will never leave.

This conduct continues today with the state welfare system, which we know of in New South Wales as the Department of Communities and Justice. Noting that different states and territories have different names for their welfare oversight, I will be referring to these bodies and practices as the department, family policing, welfare, out-of-home care, residential 'homes' and foster care.

As time has gone on, so has the practice of removing Indigenous children from our families and communities. In particular, this industry has grown through privatisation. Privatisation as a means to shift accountability. *Crossover children* is a term used to highlight the implications of crossing over, literally, from family policing and separation through to the criminal justice system.

People tend to see the alarming rates of our children going from 'care' and 'protection' to the criminal justice system. Australia as a whole nation is contributing to this pipeline – the pipeline being Aboriginal children and families being identified during the early stages of life, being subject to family policing and crossing from the family policing system to the criminal justice system. You will hear more of these yarns as the story continues.

The family policing system must be clearly called out for the outcomes we are seeing today. The child protection industry continues to make money on the back of Indigenous lives; our bodies are the data for the salary, the property and the income of all those who have a stake in this industry.

For example, in one of my foster placements I remember a deep addiction to property and money. I started to notice how the foster carers, ultimately, were taking foster children in (as many as they could) to pay off their property – using us as a quick fix to make their repayments.

Don't forget, the case worker in the department relies on removals to ensure funding continues and they are paid; the criminal justice system relies deeply on removal and the hope that our babies will become crossover children; and, of course, prison guards and corrections officers who have oversight of our kids need our kids in their systems, or else their jobs won't exist.

There is a war on Aboriginal children.

I mean it. It's the biggest industry, and it's the most harmful, using my people's bodies as a means for profit.

In recent years, the privatisation of essential public services and institutions has become a growing trend worldwide. Two major intersecting systems that have undergone significant privatisation include the prison complex and the foster care system. It is partly the reason why the term *family policing* has been coined.

By examining their privatisation, we can uncover the alarming outcomes that often arise from such practices. It becomes evident that these systems – rather than prioritising the wellbeing and rehabilitation of children and young people and supporting their families – have been transformed into profit-driven industries that exploit oppressed groups impacted by removal and incarceration. Ultimately it is systems, such as the department outsourcing their oversight to organisations, that continue to go unchecked on their conduct and behaviours.

The privatisation of prisons can be traced back to the 1980s, primarily in the United States. Driven by the notion that private companies could manage prisons more efficiently, governments began contracting out prison operations to corporations. This shift marked the beginning of a troubling era where incarceration became a lucrative business. This was mirrored globally, and now a similar system functions in Australia. There are three private operators responsible for multiple prisons in Australia: GEO Group, G4S and Serco.

Privately owned and run prisons operate on a profit motive, again for those salaries and jobs, and for income as a company. These privatised industries and companies benefit off the back of both dead and alive bodies. Australia has one of the highest rates of prisoners held in private facilities in the world.

Privately owned and run prisons rely on a steady stream of inmates – or the famous word many love, *criminality* – to generate profits. I say 'criminality' because I remember sitting in my first criminal law class at UNSW and my lecturer sharing 'there is not one definition of a criminal; we cannot simply put it into one meaning'. Yet this word is actively used to lobby for harsher sentencing laws and stricter crime policies, contributing to the phenomenon of mass incarceration. In particular, when it comes to politics, one of the biggest conversations that takes place to get voted in is how harsh you are willing to be to 'criminals' to protect the property of others. I have seen leadership respond faster to the damage of property, and inflict harsher legislation, policing powers and functions, than to Aboriginal children dying.

Towards the end of 2023, we saw Queensland suspend its *Human Rights Act* to enact a bill that allows children to be locked up in adult watch houses. Ultimately this is locking up children in adult prisons and acts as a preparatory pathway for the long term. While this may not necessarily be in the fine print, it's the intention and likely outcome when we choose to add strength to punishment instead of make appropriate changes.

The Queensland Government has introduced legislation to allow it to imprison children in police watch houses for adults, even if it would not be compatible with human rights. It's important to note the Queensland *Human Rights Act* – introduced in 2019 – protects children from being detained in adult prisons, so it had to be suspended for the government to be able to pass its legislation. This was the second instance in a single year.

What we often see in our communities is minor 'crimes' and limited legal representation resulting in the incarceration of our people. Marginalised communities, particularly First Nations people, in Australia are the most disproportionately impacted by imprisonment, and this has become a profitable enterprise.

Private prisons often cut corners to reduce costs, resulting in inadequate rehabilitation programs. The focus shifts from promoting positive change and reducing recidivism to minimising expenses. Consequently, incarcerated individuals are left without the necessary support systems to reintegrate into society successfully – or, as we horrifically know, they may be killed in custody.

Similar to the prison complex, the privatisation of the foster care system gained momentum in the late twentieth century.

Governments began outsourcing child welfare services to private agencies, believing that market competition would improve outcomes. Many of these 'market organisations' are not culturally informed (and should not have to be, as it's not their culture to learn or know) and are not Aboriginal community controlled. This means we are adding extra layers of violence when it comes to organisations determining where a First Nations child has their rightful place.

And let me tell you this: a system that is white in function cannot find the places of belonging for Black love, healing and community.

It was often stated that we needed 'community control' and our lives must be in our communities' hands, which to be honest, if that was the case in reality, would be great. However, the onus of responsibility is put into the hands of the community, but not the control and power. The funding is not direct to the community, and to this very day the department will issue grants and funding rounds for community organisations to apply for in order to support their communities. Or, when the funding is tied to community, it's with strings attached to the very same system that has enacted the abuse. In what world is it okay to say we are releasing power and control, but your abuser will continue to violently determine the final outcomes.

That's what the department does, releases tenders to communities to say, 'Yes, you fix the problems we created, but also sign here to get the full funding and say that you will work with us.' It's the 'with' for me, because the departmental system of child removal is a machine that *cannot* be worked with. It has never worked for – only against – us, and every bit of research, outcome and life we have lost prove this. Mind you, this process is also an awful one, and often the power, intellectual property and data outcomes still remain with the department.

When it comes to child removal throughout the Australian context, there has and continues to be advocacy and a fight around the importance of community-controlled organisations, which is crucial; however, often when making this drastic shift, the system places an outsized burden on the community. The department ultimately must not have oversight. The state is not a parent, not a caretaker in any way.

Despite the initial intentions, the privatisation of foster care has resulted in negative consequences for vulnerable children and families. This has occurred through financial incentives. For example, private agencies receive funding based on the number of children under their care, creating a financial incentive to keep children in the system for longer. This can lead to unnecessary removals and prolong the separation of families, ultimately benefiting the agencies financially.

In my case, I remember being with a foster placement that was completely money-driven. My vulnerable body paid off their mortgage.

They would lease the upstairs, have international students in one room, and have me in another. I remember seeing emails written from one of the foster carers to the department, saying, 'Since Vanessa is almost eighteen, she would like to go to Cambodia and help people overseas. We will need financial assistance to help her live her dreams and don't want her to miss out.'

I can promise you this, my intentions were never to go to Cambodia, but they had intentions to make profit as fast as possible before I left, as after eighteen the money foster carers receive decreases.

For many of us kids who have been through the system, we are on our own after eighteen. No support, no check-ins, and I can assure you, after the amount of visits the system did in the beginning to take you, you don't hear a word from them after they can no longer benefit off you.

I should also say, even when in the system, you are alone.

The system does not know love.

The system never loved me. The system never could.
But my people could.
My community does.

Back to privatisation and the foster care system, this often leads to reduced oversight and accountability. Private agencies may prioritise cost-cutting measures over the wellbeing of children, resulting in inadequate care and supervision. The profit motive often undermines the quality of services provided.

Just like the prison system – and throughout this book you will learn yarns about crossover children and young people – the privatised foster care system disproportionately affects marginalised communities, particularly First Nations people. Implicit biases and systemic racism contribute to higher rates of removal and placement in foster care, perpetuating cycles of oppression.

The privatisation of the prison complex and foster care system has transformed these essential public services into profit-driven industries. The prioritisation of financial gains over the wellbeing and rehabilitation of individuals has led to concerning outcomes. Mass incarceration, inadequate rehabilitation programs, exploitation of those criminalised inside prison complexes, unnecessary removals and the disproportionate impact on marginalised communities are just some of the negative consequences that arise from these intersecting systems.

It is crucial to critically evaluate and challenge the profit-driven model of these industries to ensure that the focus remains on community and keeping our jarjums (children) where they belong: with family, safety and love – not the state.

When I reflect on my story, I can't help but find myself thinking that, while we stand strong, we are continually oppressed, targeted and harmed. But the spirit that lays at our core as First Nations people is forever strong.

Even when they target us, lock us up in shackles, take us to our final breaths, remove our babies, destroy our land, our spirit is strong – we are still here and our people are always waiting for us to come home.

Our spirit and physical presence are our survival. Our spirit is why we are here.

I am not saying we don't feel pain, but our greatest weapon as Blackfullas is our spirit. It's what you don't see that will always give my people the strength, because we see this every day.

I am often not afraid when others are in a room and I am not there, because I know my old people roam these lands and waters, watching, watching it all.

Watching you, me – all of us.

Move lightly.

THE
BEGINNING

WAS JUST TEN-AND-A-HALF YEARS OLD when I was forcibly stolen from my father.

Until I was eighteen, the system took this critical time away from my family and community. A time where memories are created and stories are told between a parent and child.

This was taken from me.

But when I walk these sacred countries, I often find myself taken back to the places without concrete jungles. I remember the way our people lived in harmony, love, justice and kinship systems. I see the nature, the nurturing, the children and the elders.

And when I think of what tomorrow brings, I am reminded of what I mentioned earlier – the spirit. The power I come from, and where I am going.

For almost eight long years, I was constantly baggage moved around. I will explain the stages and how this works as you read on, but as you do, I ask you to reflect, identify and join me in learning how we can be better.

As a survivor of this system, I have learned many things. I have learned that the way forward when it comes to ending the disproportionate rate of child removal, incarceration and the continued contemporary form of enslavement is *abolition*.

I studied law and social work to try to understand this system. As a kid, I was always driven to try to understand why people do things. For me, understanding the law is important; understanding the way these systems continue to target Black families is important. My professional and personal experiences and knowledge of this system bring me to the same finding.

Abolition.

Abolition seeks out restorative practices for all. Abolition finds new ways to operate within a society that considers its members disposable.

Abolition means being there for our youth, especially young women of colour, and especially when we have a government targeting children and young people. Abolition is education in practice. It's remembering that there is a better world we can live in.

Abolition authentically serves and protects our loved ones. Abolition fights to ensure that all families have access to adequate and quality health services. Too many of my people are dying from these health systems. Racial violence is embedded in the 'Australian' way. Abolition means not having the police as first responders to mental and emotional health crises.

Abolition advocates against imprisonment and policing. Abolition does not tell people how to live their lives. Abolition is not about righteousness.

Abolition does not put us above our people and those we love. Abolition means community. It means inviting people in. It works towards repairing the friction caused by necessary separation. Honouring that it's also okay to be apart. It acknowledges enabling and provides tools to prevent this behaviour.

Abolition is about choosing the side of the community, and it is the best way to prevent and minimise harm and ensure safety for all. If we implement a new practice that is centred in care and dignity, we might find a practice that challenges our instinct to 'cancel' each other and punish the most vulnerable.

Abolition is about how we treat each other. It is about how we show up in relationships. It is about how we respond to harm caused and how we respond when we cause harm. It is differentiating between large-scale systems that have been built to perpetuate our harm, and individual harm caused against one another.

Abolition is not about bullying, but I do believe abolition is about standing up for yourself, the community and the most vulnerable and targeted.

There is a better world to reimagine, and when we actively work towards building that new world, we will bring our children home where they belong.

In our social justice work, we are often confronted with moments that test our emotional, political and personal bounds.

But when we flourish with our communities and kins, coming back to those conversations that hold us to account, we learn that we can truly reconcile what abolition means as a practice.

This feedback is critical. It allows us to reshape the work and truly move forward.

Throughout my life – my pain, grief and truth – I have embodied the following twelve principles:

1. Have courageous conversations.
2. Commit to response versus reaction. (Taught this by my Aunty Anne.)
3. Experiment and understand that nothing is fixed.
4. Say yes to one's imagination. When I was in the family policing system, I was so scared, and all I had was my imagination and my ancestors visiting.
5. Forgive actively versus passively. Do this with love. To forgive actively is about also letting go of those who

undertake harm. You do not have to stay, be with or put up with harm, unsafe circumstances or anything. But your heart and body is allowed to move forward.

6. Allow oneself to feel.
7. Commit to not harming or abusing others.
8. Practise accountability for harm caused.
9. Embrace non-reformist reforms. Recognise that this is also a step for change.
10. Build community, the ones that have kin, love and justice. Adopt our way, and we all learn and win (because the white man's way is not working and it's costing all of us). It's costing our land, soul, spirit and future.
11. Value interpersonal relationships.
12. Fight the state and do not make it stronger. That includes here in Australia and globally. I stand with Indigenous people, acknowledging our rights and purposes are intersectional.

I ask that you sit with these offerings, these principles, and create your own way forward. I hope this means you actively apply pressure and advocate on the right side of history. I hope this means you get loud. You may find me doing a formal keynote, or out in the community, but you will never find me silent.

Often, people wonder how they can show up, how they can actively listen, how they can be an ally. Maybe you have been one of these people. Maybe you have asked yourself these questions. Well, here is my answer: do not remain silent. Do something. This is what abolition is. It is choosing to *do something* with gentleness, love and justice. Or it is doing something with rightful rage, demands and accountability. All our moves interconnect together.

We need to be committed to building a culture that is rooted in care, dignity and accountability. And, right now, in these urgent times, we need people to question practices that exist. Especially those practices that are harming people.

We need people like *you* – choosing to read and learn – to demand justice for the children taken.

We need you to help us take down the family policing system that is removing our children at birth, that is seeing our children adopted out without parental consent, that is constantly regulating Black families.

We need you to use your position to write and voice support. We need you to make room for community. If you aren't Indigenous, we need you to truly understand that you are a visitor, but a visitor with the power to stand collectively for change. It also means knowing your power and asking yourself what you are willing to let go of to give power to my people, my community.

We need to build our numbers, apply pressure and let the system know that the treatment of our people is fundamental, and that prior to your legal system, we had and continue to have systems of being and doing that have existed for eternity.

We need you to believe that Black lives matter. That Black children matter. That Black mothers matter, Black healing matters, Black love matters, Black air matters, Black breaths matter. So that when officers come and take the air away from the lungs of Black bodies, and our people die in custody, you believe that it matters.

And this causes you to *do something.*

It's a deep privilege to be free from pain, trauma, violence. So, when you're tired, when you start to fall silent, remember this: I was just a kid. I was just about to close my eyes. I didn't need silence when I was ripped away. I needed someone to fight for my family and community, to fight for me.

I have never believed in replacing the current system. I do, however, believe we must abolish it. We have no choice but to radically reimagine a way of caring for children and their families. One that does not punish.

History matters.

This long yarn short isn't just my yarn. It's ours. It's one we must never forget and ensure never happens again.

To understand this yarn, you must understand the darkest features and violence that make this nation a harmful one. To understand the present, we must learn the past.

Colonisation has laid the foundations of the removal of First Nations children and young people since its very first moments. The colonial state always seeks to assert dominance and control over Indigenous lands, resources and cultures. This involved forcibly removing First Nations children from our families and communities as part of a deliberate strategy to assimilate and eradicate Indigenous culture.

It started with what many know as the Stolen Generations. These were some of the first members of our people who were directly impacted by the violence of colonisation through family separation tactics. Many did not get to come home, to country, to their families and communities.

The parallels between Indigenous child removal and enslavement are evident. As mentioned, many First Nations children and young people were taken to institutions where enslavement was enforced, often papered over with the term *domestic service*.

Both practices were employed by colonial powers to exert dominance and control over my people. Enslaved individuals were forcibly separated from their families and communities, creating deep emotional and psychological wounds that continue to reverberate through generations.

Many think slavery did not occur in Australia, but it's the foundation of the struggles we see today.

From its very first moments, invasion saw many of my people killed by the violence, displaced or stolen.

You will not meet a First Nations person across Australia who doesn't have a story or a connection to a Stolen Generations survivor or a member of their family impacted by the violence of the settler state.

The removal of First Nations children was aimed at severing their connections to their families, heritage and cultural identity, perpetuating cycles of disconnection and pain.

Many of our survivors were taken to institutions such as Cootamundra Domestic Training Home for Aboriginal Girls (1912–69). The other places in New South Wales were called Bomaderry Children's Home (1908–80) and Kinchela Boys Home (1924–70).These institutions continued their harm for a period of sixty years, from 1909 as the Aborigines Protection Board, which became the Aborigines Welfare Board in 1940, then all the way through to 1969. These systems of removal had lifelong consequences for survivors and their descendants.

While these all have the word *home* in them, they were in fact the furthest things from homes. These institutions sought to forcibly assimilate First Nations children by subjecting them to experiences of cultural erasure, abuse and trauma. The women in particular, who were sent to Cootamundra Home for Aboriginal Girls, were subjected to horrific slavery.

Throughout all these homes, many experienced sexual abuse and violence against their bodies. When we talk about the violence against our women, our elders and our people, we must not forget the intersections of violence committed against them.

Often it is our women who bear the brunt of harm, and we see that again today, with the harmful intersections of the criminal justice system targeting and disproportionately incarcerating First Nations women.

The trauma that was endured in these institutions has intergenerational consequences, as the pain and disconnection experienced by survivors is passed down to their children and grandchildren. This perpetuation of trauma further reinforces the cycles of disconnection and pain within Indigenous communities.

Often today we see generational impacts; however, the brunt of the punishment and consequences must not be on the person themselves but on the system strategically designed for what we are seeing.

Systemic biases and disparities also play a significant role in perpetuating the disproportionate representation of First Nations children in the foster care system. Historical and ongoing injustices – such as limited access to quality education, healthcare and support services – create systemic barriers that contribute to the overrepresentation of First Nations children in child welfare systems. Discriminatory practices, biases and cultural misunderstandings on the part of child welfare professionals further compound these disparities.

The historical context of Indigenous child removal is deeply intertwined with the legacies of colonisation and enslavement. The deliberate policies and practices aimed at assimilation and cultural eradication have left lasting scars on our communities.

The trauma experienced throughout the Stolen Generations contributes, in conjunction with ongoing systemic biases and disparities, to the disproportionate representation of First Nations children in the foster care and family policing system today.

Acknowledging these interconnected historical and present-day injustices is vital for a comprehensive understanding of the profound implications of family separation when advocating for meaningful change to the paternalistic system of family policing we see today.

COMMUNITY AND CHILDHOOD

THIS YARN, OR PART OF it at least, starts in Redfern, Sydney. Redfern is where my parents met. The yarn starts as they meet on Walker Street, where Dad was working for the council and Mum was one of his neighbours. One day, they ran into each other on the street. Mum was with my eldest brother, Charles, who was crying, and Dad was being cheeky with him, trying to make him smile.

He asked Mum what was wrong, and she told him, 'Oh, he just wants lollies.' So, being the kind of man my father was, he walked straight to the corner store and bought Charles some lollies. From that point on, Mum and Dad were inseparable. They had their issues at the best and worst of times, but Dad was – until he passed – Mum's confidant and biggest support. There were times when it wasn't so good, and to this day I hear different things and opinions on all of this but, no matter what, my mum literally could not live without Dad.

My middle brother, Joseph, was born not long after, and Dad continued to see the violence and harm of the policing state in Redfern. Three years later, Mum fell pregnant with me. Dad wanted to get out. He was worried about us growing up in Redfern where police were killing and literally hunting Black bodies down.

I have travelled around the world and visited many places. I have noticed that sometimes when people are asked the question 'Where are you from?' they become defensive. I especially observed this when I represented Australia at the Fourth Global Convention of Solidarity with Palestine, held in Beirut, addressing the violation of children's rights.

I had this experience with members from the Black Lives Matter movement, who were also there showing their solidarity. When I asked them where they were from, there was offence taken. I realised for some people, they are disconnected from who they are and where their people are from, but a deep fire remains to demand justice and change. Place matters, and I get that.

It was also an introduction for me to understand the nuances and differences in historical experiences from the United States and enslavement (and quite often a silence on its Indigenous people), and the First Nations context in Australia.

When I shared why I asked this, and this being part of our protocol of meeting and connecting from a First Nations perspective, they immediately realised, upset and in tears. Realising that, while subject to awful harms of colonisation, neo-imperialism and the settler state of forced displacement in their own experiences, they do actually come from a land that is different to the one they have created a physical home on in the United States. A land that has a history of stories and connection. A land that actually is not theirs but belongs to the caretakers of that land. Indigenous lands.

The intersectional differences of identity and connection to place are unique to many individuals. However, here in Australia, I find that the question 'Where are you from?' is a way for Indigenous people to connect in our resistance and shared experiences. When I am asked this, I feel safe, because it's a moment to share. This is not meant to offend but rather to find our place, our stories and our truths. Who are your ancestors? Where do your song lines begin? Who are your people?

The rhythm of the land keeps our spirits strong. The land holds stories and strength. White people may use Google Maps for direction, but we rely on our song lines and stories for generational survival. Our song lines are our sacred places, our kinship and our understanding of how to live, act and feel. This includes our connection to animals, trees and all things natural. This is who we are, beyond any mapping tool.

The violence of colonisation has disturbed this way of life. But still, it remains in how we practise our sovereignty and love for each other. Our stories, together, are what keep our past alive for our future.

So, when we ask the question 'Where are you from?' we are connecting. Among Indigenous people, this question is one of the most important ways for us to come together and share a common understanding of our experiences as Indigenous people. It is also a way to reconnect with our family ties and mend any cracks that may exist due to colonisation.

When we ask each other this question, we are not being rude. I understand that many people may not know where they are from, but rather than getting defensive, it could be an invitation to learn about your roots or gently explore why you may not know. Stories matter, and where your story begins is significant.

Here you'll have a little of my long yarn short.

I am a proud Bundjalung Widubul-Wiabul woman, deeply rooted in my identity and heritage. We are the saltwater people. We are also freshwater people, where we have rivers, mountains and stories that interconnect.

My life began in Sydney on Gadigal country, where I was born at the Royal Hospital for Women, which is built on Bidjigal country. The true beginning goes back many years earlier, to Bundjalung country, the land of my people. These stories belong not only to me but also to a history of pain and resistance, and to ongoing narratives shared by many who walk these lands and waters. The term *country* holds the essence of survival and connection. It's a place to always come back home to.

Country is often not understood by the Western world, and that's okay. It's not meant for them. However, if they respected the land and the place they benefit from, the world would be different.

The circumstances surrounding my birth foreshadowed what was to come and echoed the experiences of my family for generations. Instead of joy and celebration, my birth brought anxiety to my mother. For many First Nations families, the healthcare system is not safe – let alone the people working within it.

My mother had already given birth to two sons, Charles and Joseph. Charles had been forcibly removed from my mum during his later childhood years. She had experienced the pain of that loss and the stress of trying to keep him out of the system, which he was in and out of from that moment on.

With my birth came another opportunity for loss, for another child to be stolen.

I was born to two parents who were battling their own demons. But I was also born into a family and community full of love, fiercely protective of its children.

My mum was diagnosed with schizophrenia at a young age. The remarkable thing about her is that she had insight and knowledge about her mental illness, even though she never received proper support or education. She could recognise when manic episodes were happening and when she was becoming unwell. My mum had a painful upbringing of her own, where she experienced physical, sexual and emotional abuse.

In this context, let me tell you that when it comes to illness, here in Australia, mental illness is seen as consent to be controlled, demeaned and treated as if you don't matter. Often the response to my mum's illness was discriminatory, as she was viewed as incapable of doing what needed to be done or fulfilling society's expectations of her.

But in my world, she was my mum, my everything. That's the beauty of being a child; you only see the love in your parents and other adults. It's a vulnerable time in which you don't really understand what is good or bad. And that's heartbreaking to think about.

When I reflect on how Mum was treated, especially now as an adult, it becomes clear to me how badly she was failed by the system on many intersecting accounts. If someone arrives at the hospital with a broken leg, they are treated with care. But when you come with a mental illness, you often don't receive the primary support you need.

For Mum, her mental illness was something she constantly battled and managed, knowing that it was one of the ways the system could justify taking her children away from her. Sadly, this hasn't changed today. Her illness was used against her to justify the removal of my siblings and me, and there is no world in which this is acceptable.

To me, Mum was much more than her schizophrenia. She had various jobs over the years, including serving ice-cream on the beach. My grandparents owned the ice cream truck. She would serve ice cream down at Coogee Beach (which means *smelly beach*). She also worked in the baggage unit at the airport and trained as a nurse at the former Prince Henry Hospital in Little Bay. Growing up in Merro-berah (later changed to *Maroubra*), Mum was a child of the ocean and an outstanding surfer. She was a triplet, and my grandparents, Pop Lindsey and Nan Valerie, raised their children in public housing, just as my own parents did. Pop Lindsey fought in the Vietnam War, and the PTSD he suffered meant that he was never quite the same again. Mum was one of eight.

My father, Alby Roberts, was a Bundjalung man who carried the burden of generational trauma. His great-grandmother, May Brown, was a victim of slavery and displacement. His grandfather, Alby Roberts (whom my father was named after), was a professional boxer who fought throughout the North Coast and Australia. He was something of a legend and was nicknamed 'Poison'.

Pop Alby travelled across these sacred lands and waters, fighting both physically as a boxer and spiritually and mentally to survive as a Black man in a colony where the systems were designed to diminish his life, extinguish his spirit and erase him from these lands.

He was also one of the very few Black people who travelled internationally at the time. This was only possible after he was granted exemption by the white man to do so. An exemption order was a policy enforced by state governments on some Aboriginal people during the twentieth century in Australia. It was enacted through a single clause included in many of the 1909 so-called 'protection' acts, which controlled the lives, decisions and wellbeing of my people.

The exemption orders allowed government administrators to declare some individual First Nations people to be 'exempt' from the legislation, like my Pop Alby. This wasn't a blessing, though – it reminded him and all Black people that our choices were down to the 'permission' of the white man. And it in no way meant being free from racism, institutional abuse and the ongoing violence of the colony. Can you imagine that? Being on your own lands and having to ask permission to do anything.

Well, that is what Australia did to my people, and if I am being honest here, it's something that has not stopped. Tools like the requirement for permission and consent from institutions and other bodies continue to be enforced on my people.

One generation later, my Pop Collin Roberts married Hazel Roberts. I feel the spirit of Nan Hazel through me, I feel her so deeply, and Pop Collin was my best friend growing up. On weekends we would always bake dinners for lunch at Pop's. We would head over Saturday afternoon, all of us grandchildren, acting like we were WWE superstars, watch the scariest movies you could think of, and bring out the beds to lay out in the lounge room and snuggle up.

By Sunday morning, Pop Collin would wake up as early as Grandfather Sun to get ready for our baking. He always kept a cold South Sydney Rabbitohs glass in the freezer. Always a cold glass available for his beverage, after feeding and looking after all his grandchildren. I remember this being one of the earliest memories of safety. The smell, the cook-ups, the love that came with our kin and being together. I loved being together. This was a place of connection, of safety with our bellies full.

These are some of my favourite memories as a child. Just coming together at Pop's and being together. As a child, it was all I knew really.

Pop Collin loved having his babies at home. Early in the morning, I would be the first to wake, and my uncle had all of his instruments at home. An acoustic guitar, piano, bass guitar, electric guitar. As soon as the sun came up, I would get up and run straight to the instruments. I would start playing music so loud in the hope that I would be able to wake somebody else up to come and play. Pop would quietly and gently get up and say, 'Bubba, everyone is sleeping.' He then would give me five or ten dollars to stop playing.

There was and is something safe about being with your cousins and family as a kid. It grounds you, and this is one of the experiences of growing up Black – you stay surrounded by family. I had all of this – my family, community, my safety. But white institutions, like child protection systems, they don't see the connection and kinship. They see it as 'overcrowding' or 'unsafe', and they don't try to understand the cultural difference. In my field of work, I have seen individuals in professions such as teaching make comments to child protection systems that children are unsafe because they are sharing a bed.

One story I was told was about a Koori child. (*Koori* is a term you will read quite often in my writing; it's what we call us mob from New South Wales.) When this child returned to school after the October long weekend, he mentioned sleeping on the floor with his cousins. A teacher made a Risk of Significant Harm Report to the department, also known as ROSH reporting, stating he was unsafe and being neglected.

When it was investigated, and thankfully a First Nations educator who was aware of our ways saw it first, it came out that the October long weekend was the time of one of the biggest Indigenous events in New South Wales: the Koori Knockout, which is where all our communities come together and often families share their homes.

When it's a Black family, it's neglect, and urgent state intervention is needed, but when it's a white family having a family weekend, it's all cute, they are all sharing.

This could have resulted in that young Koori child being removed and his whole family torn apart. That is the reality of a system that does not understand our ways at all.

When I was at my pop's, this is what we did back then. It was a happy time, surrounded by the people I loved and in the culture I understood with my family and community.

This early part of my life was spent in Redfern, Sydney. Redfern has always been known to Black people as a meeting place – whether you're travelling down south or going up north, you can always find connection and place within Redfern.

To many non-Indigenous people, Redfern was and often still is considered dangerous. This is racism. As First Nations people growing up in this area, the only people we knew to be dangerous were the police. The rate of crime at this time on Gadigal country (Redfern) was increasing. The rates of police brutality and abuse were significantly high, and just like we see today in the midst of our gentrified communities and places, the abuse still takes place.

The thing is, Redfern has always been a place of resistance. It has always been held as a place of both historical and contemporary resistance in the Black movement. This has been power to our people and power of place. While the gentrifying continues, you can also see the way many Black folks remain or pass through.

For many people from the North Coast, such as Bundjalung country, Dunghutti and the other sacred countries up north, when invasion occurred, many members came down to Gadigal country – Redfern. This continues to be an act of resistance.

Pop Collin, who used to drive the trucks from Gadigal to the north, and Nan Hazel made Redfern part of their home and lived on Walker Street and Mary Street. These are the housing estates, next to what many know as 'the suicide towers'. These towers are built just like prisons. They are suffocating – just a small square and so far from the ground. They are mostly made up of my people, and that is the most heartbreaking thing: to put our people as far away from the land as possible and create a sense of imprisonment in the faulty-made housing estates.

It didn't get its nickname for no reason. Many of our people have died in those towers, either by suicide or by police pursuit over balconies, the severity of the height of the towers often resulting in death.

Redfern is historically known and still known today to be incredibly racist and harmful. My father tells me the story of when the police put him in lockup. When inside, the police stuck their fingers up his nose and dragged him out, calling him a 'black coon' and intimidating him in front of the other officers as they laughed at my dad and treated him like an animal.

Even as an adult, when my dad would struggle, I would hear him speak in his sleep and sleepwalk, making comments about the treatment he had endured over the course of his life. This place is truly violent.

When I was about two years old, we were successful in a housing transition application, so off we moved to the housing commission flat in Bilga. Bilga is on the lands of Bidjigal people. People there are strong, particularly the area being very close to Botany Bay, where invasion first took place. La Perouse, which is a strong Black community, also became part of my community and family as a child.

As a kid, I loved being around the older children. I was known as the baby of the group, always the youngest but also the most daring. I wanted to be just like my older brother Joseph, so I would tag along with him, his friends and our cousins. My dad would say that I could only go out if Joseph was watching me. It used to drive my brother mad.

Joseph has always been my caretaker. He worries about me and always wants me to be okay. Even now, he messages me and says, 'Bub, your happiness means everything to me. Promise me you're okay.'

Having a brother like Joseph, who is always there for me no matter what he's going through, is something special. Despite the struggles and losses we faced as kids and adults, we continue to support each other. Don't get me wrong, we are also prepared to growl each other too.

My brother Joseph is a gentle giant, and he is faced with his own struggles.

We grew up next to a place we called 'Black Road'. It was a steep road at the back with bushes next to our housing units. We used to ride little PeeWee 50s through the bush, causing mischief. One time, we ventured a bit further and discovered a set of big containers. As kids, we made up stories about them, saying that ghosts, or 'goonges' in our lingo, lived there. Beyond that, there was a space filled with what we thought was clay, so we named it 'Clay World'.

One day, we decided to play there. But security saw us and chased us through the bush, all the way to a little pond between the housing area and the wealthier section up the road. We ran as fast as we could and had no choice but to jump into the pond. What I didn't realise was that it was quicksand – or 'quickmud'. My feet got stuck and it started dragging me down.

A cousin friend suggested to my brother that they should leave me there to escape security. However, my brother said, 'No way ... My dad will give me a hiding if I don't come back with her.' He got help from a golf player nearby, and he used the golf club to pull me out.

That moment reminded me of three things. First, my brother knew he had to take care of me because he feared our dad's response. Second, the term 'quick' in quicksand is not an exaggeration; it drags you down fast. And third, us Black kids can run faster than security.

The police always targeted my brother in our community. He was always stopped for a 'random' search by police and treated as a second-class citizen. The policing system in our community is known for targeting the vulnerable, but not due to being 'criminal' – due to having a mental illness and, when episodes occur, being punished. I remember many nights at Maroubra Police Station, begging them to take him to a hospital for help instead of police stations and holding cells.

Joseph now lives in a housing commission property, and my dream is to one day buy him a beautiful apartment, free from the noise and chaos that seems is always around him.

I went to a daycare and preschool in La Perouse called Gajuga. Gajuga was the best. It was the cultural school for all us Koori kids.

I have memories of never sleeping when the other kids slept (it's probably why I am so tired now … or I haven't changed at all – many of my community and friends call me Turbo).

Uncle Dave, who is a respected community member, would pick us up every morning on the community bus. He would beep, and all the Koori kids would come running out. To this day, I still know the beep of Uncle Dave picking us all up.

Aunty Petra, who ran the daycare and is from the community, nourished us as children. She loved us like her very own and was a source of strength for so many of us. Even now, as an adult, when I see Aunty Petra, she is still the same most loving human.

This is something that still hurts me to this day, the memories that were also taken when I was stolen. I remember being raised so strongly in our culture and community.

I was and am so proud. But, at the age of ten, the system truly attempted to take that away from me.

My dream was also to get Mum and Dad out of housing and set them up once I earned some cash and was in the position to do so. I remember when I was little, I just wanted to be able to buy my mum a new pair of shoes. She always had secondhand clothing. To be honest, she rocked it like a superstar, but I just wanted to spoil her when I could and give back.

Long yarn short, you know what annoys me about today? The way rich people love 'thrifting' and those with incomes love going to places like Vinnies and secondhand clothing stores. Let me be real, when we were kids, this was not cool. In fact, this is all we had access to afford and if our clothes were not decent, the wealthy kids reminded us. Now the rich and middle-class people go in and shop for secondhand clothing and take what is decent from someone who may not be able to afford it, instead of shopping elsewhere.

It's now really cool to look broke. But let me be real again: if you are broke, Black and a First Nations child, you have a risk of removal. Trust me. I see kids, families and communities who come from low income or poverty missing out ... again.

I attended Malabar Primary School, a local school in our community that most of us Koori kids went to. I was enrolled in Malabar from Kindergarten to Year 5. Unfortunately, in my final year of primary school, I was uprooted and forced to change schools when I was stolen from my family. It was a tumultuous time for me, and my dad played a huge role in providing support and love during this difficult period. He would visit me regularly at school, checking for any signs of abuse and ensuring that I was well-fed.

There was one teacher at Malabar, Aunty Leanne. My dad had a great love for her, as did everyone else at the school. Aunty Leanne was aware of Dad's visits and never reported him to the department. She understood the bond we shared and knew that my dad meant no harm. Unfortunately, the department eventually discovered this arrangement, leading to my removal from the only stable environment I knew at that time. However, I had another teacher named Ms Eaton during this difficult period who tirelessly advocated for me to remain at Malabar until the end of Year 5. Ms Eaton's dedication to her students was undeniable.

Amid the upheaval, I found myself at Narwee Primary School, starting my final year of primary education while in foster placements. It was a daunting experience, but I was determined to face it head-on. I encountered a bully, a white classmate, who was tasked with showing me around the school. Unfortunately, she took advantage of this opportunity to bully me and talk behind my back. This is when I crossed paths with Nadia, who would later become one of my closest friends. Nads, as I call her, stood up for me and put an end to the bullying. She invited me into her friendship circle, and although we eventually went to different high schools, we remained in contact.

Nads is truly one of the most remarkable individuals I have encountered in this world. When I was in an abusive home that restricted my access to extended family, Nads helped me plan ways to see my kin. She was familiar with the area where my uncle lived, providing me with the necessary directions on buses and trains. Nads and I would skip school together, embarking on these journeys to see my family. It was a rare moment of freedom in a life that often felt restrained and monitored. The ability to spend time with my kin was something I cherished, as it was limited for me under the watchful eye of the system. Case workers constantly reminded me that seeing my parents once a month was a privilege and that each time I saw them I was depriving another child of their visitation rights. These statements broke me.

For high school, I attended Beverly Hills Girls High School, which was known for its diverse student population. We had a significant number of Lebanese, Palestinian, Pasifika and Indigenous students. We also had a variety of religions at our school too, from Muslim to Christian to Buddhist. Most lunch times, and before school, I admired watching students of the Muslim faith undertake the prayer. Looking back, white kids were actually the minority in our school.

Adjacent to our school was an Intensive English Centre (IEC), which newly arrived students would attend before transitioning to high school. I loved spending time with the students from the IEC. I would often arrive early to school just to hang out with this mob, or I would invite them to play on the courts at our high school. During the Year 7 orientation, I watched the school leaders on the stage, including the school and sports captains. I envisioned myself one day standing among them during assemblies. As I familiarised myself with the school system, I realised that I didn't aspire to become school captain, because it seemed like a position that involved attending tea events and boasting about the school without making a significant impact on the students. Instead, I set my sights on becoming sports captain.

When I turned fifteen, in Year 9, I initiated a campaign called Change the Conversation. This was birthed out of a program I attended with the National Indigenous Youth Leadership Academy. This campaign aimed to promote solidarity between diverse groups and challenge the harmful narratives that targeted our diverse community. Change the Conversation united the entire school and fostered a sense of togetherness among us. It focused on advocating for the rights of refugees.

In Year 10, I witnessed the challenges faced by the students transitioning from the IEC to high school, which inspired me to create a program called Just for Kicks. Just for Kicks focused on fostering connections through open conversations, mental health support and sports. The program aimed to bring together Pasifika, First Nations and Middle Eastern students, as well as other students of colour, but welcomed everyone.

As someone who had to adapt to new environments and learn to connect with new people constantly, I recognised the power of human connection. Fridays were particularly tough for me because, like many others, I didn't know what to expect over the weekend. In collaboration with a supportive physical education teacher who dedicated her time to supervising the program, we organised Just for Kicks for every Friday during lunchtime and two hours after school. We shared meals, had meaningful conversations encompassing the good, the bad and the better, played sports, and most importantly never neglected the care and support we provided for each other. Word of mouth spread about our program, and Samsung even sponsored it. We had a short video created and received funding for food supplies and sporting equipment.

In my final year of high school, I was elected sports captain, and I cherished the opportunity to be someone others could confide in. Creating a safe space was always my primary goal. As I approached seventeen, I realised that the people who were meant to care for me didn't truly do so. I was the first in my family to go beyond Year 9 and the first to graduate in the foster family placement I had been taken to. However, nobody came to celebrate Year 12 graduation with me. It was an incredibly heartbreaking moment that I still vividly remember. I watched as other families turned up for their children and siblings, and I walked down to collect my graduation certificate with shame and a deep pain in my heart.

The foster carers didn't attend because they simply didn't care, and I believe they were uncomfortable with the fact that even their own children hadn't progressed past Year 10. How could a First Nations kid with trauma manage to finish Year 12?

My parents didn't come because they believed they wouldn't be allowed to attend due to the consistent silencing they had experienced throughout the years. Everyone made my parents feel like they didn't have a place. I would have given anything to have them there with me.

In the absence of those who were supposed to be there, my physical education teacher showed me love and support by being present. To this day, I hold her dear to my heart. We do not speak often anymore, but her being there meant so much. I cannot tell you how important teachers are in our world. The good ones exist.

While I often felt neglected during pivotal moments in my life, I found solace in art. Art provided me with freedom and an outlet for expression. From the age of twelve, I immersed myself in the world of theatre through the Shopfront. Shopfront was owned and run by young people like me, and I was fortunate to receive a scholarship to perform there. I fell in love with writing, acting and filming. The walls of the Carlton Shopfront theatre witnessed the pain that resided within me. Art always carries political undertones, even if we don't realise it, and it became my sanctuary. In this space, I wasn't surrounded by case workers, foster carers or people constantly highlighting the faults in my parents and the complications in my life. Instead, I found a place where my young self could make sense of the world and share my experiences. I could just be a kid with an imagination. It was a place where I could make sense externally of everything that was not making sense inside of me.

Art gave me a sense of belonging.

Art provided a safe haven.

When you are a kid stolen, confused or subject to any form of detachment, for that matter, you learn not to attach yourself to things, and that I truly worked on. I get scared to get comfortable with people – it takes me a while to lend my heart – but you'll always have my respect first. Being stolen changes your life forever.

This is not just history. This is right now.

STOLEN

I REMEMBER.

I want you to imagine being a kid, just about to close your eyes, and you feel the energy of fear and anxiety enter the home. You hear the sound of your dad going onto the balcony. You know that he is terrified; he knows what is about to happen. He yells, 'Bub … Big girl … I am so sorry, but they are coming to get you.' I know. He knows.

It's like we've been waiting for this moment since I was born.

I was just a kid. I was just about to close my eyes, and Dad had tucked me into bed. But those were the last moments where I was safe, where I was home.

Everything was okay, until it wasn't.

Over twelve police officers and a case worker descended on our house. I could hear the loud knocking on our door. A voice booming, 'Open up, Alby. We are here to take Vanessa.' No cloaking the truth, no trying to soften it.

My dad was a gentle Black man who was extremely fearful of police and their brutality against our people. He was terrified.

I remember walking out to the living room after I heard the knock on the door. I was terrified too. My gut knew that something was about to happen.

'Hug your dad one last time … You are coming with us,' I was told.

I began to hug my dad. I began to cry and scream. I didn't want to leave Dad. I didn't want to leave.

I screamed.

My whole body was in shock.

I didn't want to go.

Dad … Dad … Dad …

Police came from behind, and as I felt Dad hold me tighter and closer, I felt the tears run down my cheek.

The police took my hands from where they were tightly holding on to Dad, ripping me away.

My hands were held behind my back by the police, as if I were a criminal.

I was just a kid, placed into the care of DOCS – the Department of Community Services. They forced me down the stairs, still holding my hands behind my back.

They were dragging me as I resisted. I was scared.

Neighbours were watching what was happening; they heard my screaming. I was broken in every way.

I was forced into the back of the vehicle.

I cried so much that I vomited.

To this day, my reaction when I am triggered with anxiety or memory is to vomit. Often my body responds prior to my mind catching up. I also dissociate, to this day, by sleeping.

I remember looking outside the window of the kidnappers' car. It was raining, and to this day when I see the rain, I am reminded.

This was only the first moment in a series of what would become terrifying memories that haunt me still.

Everything was okay until it wasn't.

Because they deemed my father unsuitable to care for me, the department immediately stated that my mum was also unsuitable. Mum was completely well and, although she sometimes struggled with her mental health, there was absolutely no reason why she could not have been supported to care for me (nor why my father couldn't have been equally supported).

The night I was stolen, my big brother Joseph was with Mum. My brother is also very intuitive, and it was like he knew something was about to happen. I was a bit confused by why he wanted to go to Mum's, but also I know he loved being at Mum's too. I didn't think much of it, but I knew he didn't like the drinking.

As a kid, I remember just wanting to save Dad, and if I am honest, no child should feel this for their parents, but when they are your parents, you will do anything.

Some people just need a hand, and nobody was giving that to Dad. I really needed the other adults in the world to be the adults.

My removal was in the works from the moment I was conceived. They started surveilling our family from this moment. Especially my mum.

For most pregnant people, when you are carrying your baby, the experience is meant to be one of joy, one where you should be able to hear things like 'Congratulations!' and 'How far along are you? When are you due?'

These questions are the common ones.

That's how it should be, right?

But for my mother, her pregnancy was filled with fear. Her mental health was a constant battle – one she was still learning to self-manage. She really needed support, but this was not forthcoming, not from the health system or social workers. She had already had one child removed, and she was anxious the whole time she was pregnant with me that I would be next. Sadly, these anxious worries were proven to be true.

Her pregnancy was a vulnerability, and her child (me) was used against her to punish her. Stealing a mother's child will break anybody.

Giving birth should also be a time of joy, and hospitals places of safety and support. But my parents had the opposite experience. From the moment I was born, their experience was one of being watched, social workers visiting, over-servicing and the discrimination they attracted by virtue of my father being an Aboriginal man and my mother living with a mental illness.

For so many Black families, hospitals are not safe. They are tools of the state and are seen as policing institutions. These tools are in the midwives, the social workers, the doctors, the eyes on the walls that are meant to be for your safety. They can be racist settings, adding to the harm of your body and the circumstances.

When it comes to reproduction and the autonomy of our bodies, often these places are harmful towards our people and children. I know for a fact my mum felt this. My mum was constantly disempowered her whole life.

As I read my case files now as an adult, I come across some minutes relating to my mum and dad in a 'conference' meeting with the department. My mum was telling stories of how I was as a child. She said things like, 'Vanessa was always a healthy baby. She was so good.'

I read this and cannot help but reflect that, eleven years later, my mum was sitting in a room full of case workers talking about me as a baby. My mum was sharing with them that she did know about me and my childhood, that she was aware of how I was and the fact that I was a good child was a reflection on her parenting.

I credit my mum for the person I am today, not only because I am a mother myself, but also because I know now that those early stages of life set the foundation.

My mum, till the last moments I was with her, held my hand with love and pain together. She was still so scared of everything being taken from her. Sadly, she was taken from me in the end – suicide. She didn't commit suicide; she died by suicide and systems failure. To this day, formally there has been no cause of death described on her death certificate. This is because we are currently awaiting legal inquest processes. It has been over five years and still no movement. We continue to wait, wait, wait. Part of me feels like a whole lifetime has happened in between.

My heart cannot let my mother's death go. Why? Because others continue to face the same struggle. I see the way the system places such a burden on families, with the struggle to seek justice, answers, accountability.

An inquest does not give us justice, and sadly I know this from many experiences of supporting the community through these times, but what it does give is a chance to identify processes and to hold those people who played a role in the injustice of the death to account. It matters, but my goodness we are tired. I am tired. I want answers, I want change, and that's why I'm going through this process. The administrative burden on the actual system is worth it; they must be accountable and reflective, and they must learn – and I really hope that when the next person calls for help, they do better.

The most difficult thing I find about all of this is the way my mum was completely silenced from the start.

My poor mum.

The thing is, my mum was very intuitive and managed her mental illness carefully. Growing up, us kids would move between Dad's and Mum's; they lived five minutes away from one another in Bilga. Our parents co-parented in a more open, flexible way than could be understood by the Western ideas of parenting. My parents loved each other deeply, but equally they loved each other enough to know that being separated can sometimes be for the better. No matter what, though, my dad had my mum's back, and vice versa. He continued to take her shopping, always ensured Joseph was okay, and looked after Mum and her mental health when needed.

And besides our parents, there were aunties and uncles, our pop, cousins and a whole community who shared responsibility for each other.

It was love and culture, but to the system it looked like kids running around without clear adult supervision, like neglect.

Mental illness looked incapable.

Being a Black man looked violent and inadequate.

Again, there was no reason why Mum could not take me the night I was stolen, or why someone could not call my aunty to come to our home and check in instead of the police, especially during that traumatic removal. To this day, I have nightmares about the police putting my hands behind my back and I feel my dad's tears on my cheek.

To completely remove my mum, the woman who birthed me, who loved me, who cared for and nourished my wellbeing, was the most heartbreaking thing for both me and her. I can only imagine how she would have been feeling. To think she was treated as incapable and not allowed the care and permanence of her daughter is a disgrace on the department's part, and they should be ashamed of their conduct.

I remember as an adult reading a case note and seeing how the system had done so much damage to our family that Mum could see the pain in me. Mum was quoted in the case notes: 'Big girl ... Vanessa will only see me as a friend and that's okay. She won't know me as her mother because you took her from me.'

I remember breaking down reading this. Mum was and always will be my mum. I have never forgotten what made being eighteen so special. Those few years I got back with her, to hold her hand, to share a tea together, to laugh and hear some yarns. But make no mistake, I believe the department, its trauma on her body and the pain it put her through, played an active role up until the moment she suicided. The trauma, the pain, the harm coming back.

Thinking about it now, I'm just so angry and hurt. I'm angry at the time taken away from my family, angry at the way that my mother doesn't get to be here for her granddaughter now. I'm hurt that when I read my case files and see the way my mother was silenced, I can clearly see how she was discriminated against for her mental illness.

When I read the reports and see that they'd already decided that Mum wasn't suitable to look after me, even while she may have held some hope that she would be, it hurts because Mum has always known what's best for me.

Every mother knows their child, just like I know my daughter. I know what works and what doesn't work, and maybe sometimes along the way I might get it wrong, but we work it out. That's what parenting is a lot of the time, and most people are lucky to be able to have these learning moments, this trial and error, without being judged as bad parents and without the fear of their child being taken away.

The reality is my parents were denied every chance possible.

I remember losing my mum like it was yesterday. I have always known survival and what it takes to get through things. I had to learn this as a kid – very fast. With no choice.

I was in my class for social work at uni. Going back to what I had control of was always the important thing for me: my studies, and ensuring I work my arse off so I don't fall and break. I was doing my presentation, numb, just surviving. Until there was a knock at the door.

It was two people dressed quite formally. My stomach immediately turned to knots. They asked for me to come outside. I did.

We walked up to Nura Gili, the First Nations centre on campus. Part of me was excited to hear mum had been admitted, that she was getting help. I felt a moment of relief … until that was not the news at all.

They were there to tell me that Mum had suicided. That she had jumped from the top balcony floor. I asked why no-one came when I called … I asked about timings, I asked about everything I could.

I broke. Shattered. I could not move.

Writing this I break a little more. But the yarn matters.

So much.

At that point, I am broken. I wonder every day whether those parts will come together again.

In the time since I lost my parents, from 2017 till now, I graduated law school. I completed a social work degree, honours, had my beautiful daughter and was appointed to positions I could only ever imagine.

I will be honest. Nothing changes the foundation of a broken injustice attached to death. Nothing. I hold my daughter and I look to her hands. I see the lines of love she comes from, the lines of love she is, and the ancestors protecting her.

I look at the world I am creating in my home, and I am proud of that. Knowing that the opportunities I have worked my arse off for are changing the narrative for the world that was systemically set out for me the moment I was born.

But it does not change a broken heart, two parents taken by injustices and the continued harm faced by our people. It's ongoing.

My mum knew more than anyone the fear of the department.

Mum was always someone who provided for others. I remember when we were kids, all the other kids in our street loved coming to our place. They would often wait for me to come outside and play, and then say, 'Can we go up to your house?' Mum would have the lollies and food ready for all the kids in our street. She loved making sure we all had something to eat, always wanting to make sure our bellies were full.

I'm not unaware of the way Mum struggled, though. She had to face things in society that are completely unbearable. As a young woman in the 1980s, Mum had to endure things like an illegal abortion because there was no way to have a safe one with proper medical care. She had to learn to manage her schizophrenia in a time when it was even more stigmatised and misunderstood than it is now.

When Mum first became pregnant with my oldest brother, Charles, I know she struggled. Charles's father had lied to her, and it was only when she became pregnant that she discovered he was married and had a whole family of his own. But Mum rose to the challenge and raised my brother for the majority of his early childhood alone.

However, with her mental illness and the trauma she was dealing with, the system took it upon itself to profile my mother, and they took my biggest brother. The violence and trauma inflicted on my family by the department was only just starting.

I have said before that the safest place for a child is in the womb. That is the reality. However, even as I write this, I also note that it becomes the most dangerous place for that child as well.

Pregnancy is a time when our bodies are surveilled by health professionals, and there is a risk of significant harm from Risk of Significant Harm (ROSH) reporting, leading to the department profiling mothers and having them on their radar. ROSH reporting is often used to justify a mandatory report, and of course, if you are Indigenous, the risk is escalated.

I remember when I was carrying my daughter, Waitui, the fear that I had inside me every time I would have to go for a check-up; every time I would have to go and ensure that everything was okay. I feared she would be stolen from me.

Other pregnant people look forward to these visits – a chance to learn about their baby and to hear how they're doing in the womb. For me, I carried the legacy of my trauma, the fear of what these people could think and then write about me and what that could mean for my child.

When it comes to First Nations people, the health system is inherently racist. The same places that are meant to be for our safety, health and protection are, in fact, some of the most dangerous places for a First Nations person.

These places historically have always held deep pain. The hospital setting, as a whole, has acted as party to the removal, ongoing negligence and deaths that our people continue to face. The constant act of pathologising and over-servicing First Nations people has resulted in more pain and negative outcomes.

The lives of First Nations children in Australia continue to be disproportionately impacted by statutory out-of-home care. First Nations children are eleven times more likely than non-Indigenous children to be placed into out-of-home care.

The number of Aboriginal and Torres Strait Islander children in out-of-home care rose from 52.5 per thousand children in 2014 to 59.4 per thousand children in 2018. This comes from the Australian Institute of Health and Welfare, where we continue to see failure to meet any of the targets that could change the narrative for our people.

In 2017 and 2018, Aboriginal and Torres Strait Islander children aged between five and nine were 13.2 times as likely as their non-Indigenous peers to be in out-of-home care nationally, while those aged between fifteen and seventeen were 8.9 times as likely.

Family regulation and policing First Nations communities are among the predominant features that contribute to these higher rates. As I shared earlier in this yarn, it starts with the surveillance of families, regulating what they deem is the right way, the only way. It's a system designed perfectly to do what it is doing right now.

I am not naive to the harms. I knew harm because I also knew love; I knew when I was unsafe because I knew safety. When things were good in my family they were really good, but sometimes they weren't. Here is my earliest memory.

I am under the table. I look to the grey-and-black couch. I see the needle, the arm and the lady laying there knocked out. She's on heroin. The needle is stuck in her arm. She's knocked out cold.

I'm still under the table. I see my big brother, Joseph, a little distance away. He looks at me. He has always been my protector. I then see my other big brother, Charles, rushing in. He pulls me out from under the table, holds me tight and takes me to safety. He saves me that night.

You see, I was just two-and-a-half years old; I am now twenty-seven writing this memory as my body holds the moment I witnessed this and what my little body had to hold on to in order to survive.

You might be thinking, where were my mum and dad? I am not sure either. I was left in the drug house under the table. Anything could've happened.

I know that in that moment it should not have been my eldest brother, Charles, saving me and my other brother, Joseph, who would have been five at the time.

I know all these things are wrong, but still, as a kid, as an adult right now, all I wanted was for my parents to get help. I just wanted them supported. I just wanted to not be subject to a place where all odds were against my whole family.

I want to take you back to that night when I was stolen from my father's house by strangers. I want you to think about how confusing and traumatising it is for a child to watch her father cry and have to listen to the authority of complete strangers when it goes against everything she's been taught.

We were raised our whole lives not to go with strangers. And yet, that night, I was taken by strangers, put in the back of a strange car and taken to a strange house, all without really understanding what was happening and with no chance for Dad to explain it or comfort me.

When you are removed from your family by the state, the first place you go is 'emergency care'. This is basically a temporary foster care arrangement while the department finds potential 'suitable carers' and the case goes to court.

The protocol for Indigenous children is outlined in the Aboriginal Child Placement Principle. The principle has been endorsed in legislation or policy in all Australian states and territories. But the evidence shows it's failing our children and it's failing to reach its own set objectives.

One of the biggest failures in this system is its failure to listen to children and understand what wellbeing is to them.

The department simply has not caught up with identifying the needs of children, but rather it focuses on punishing families.

I want you to put yourself back into my shoes for a moment.

Imagine you are only ten-and-a-half years old, growing up in your community, connected deeply to your family and culture.

You live in social housing, and you know you are a little bit different to the rest of the privileged world, but in your mind, you are rich. You are rich in the love of your parents – no matter how broke they are, your plate is always filled and your stomach is always nourished.

At times, your clothes are a bit dirty, and yeah, there are circumstances where you should have been safer. But the care in your community stretches beyond just your parents, and there is always someone looking out for you.

The system could recognise this – it could acknowledge that there is so much good in your life, and that where things may break down or falter, all that's needed is more support for your parents, for the other adults in the community doing their best despite poverty and racism creating endless challenges. But instead of the system providing support and love to family, community or kin, you are stolen in the middle of the night by police officers and a case worker.

When I was taken, I was completely bewildered. A lot of the actual movements of those first few years feel hazy to me, but I know that I went through multiple short-term foster care placements before a permanent place was found for me when I was around eleven or twelve, where I stayed until I was eighteen.

When you're in the foster system, you generally have maybe one backpack's or garbage bag's worth of belongings that you're allowed to take from home – if there is time, that is. They might just rip you away to get you to the car as quickly as possible.

You're often handed an envelope by your case worker when you arrive at a new place and told to give it to your new carers. The envelope will have around $50 in it to cover any immediate costs before the system sorts out their payments for the placement. I remember that one of the common things foster carers would do is use the money to buy head-lice shampoo, because there was this assumption I'd have nits and that I was a dirty kid.

To this very day, I think this is why I shampoo and condition my hair every night, have to shower twice a day and am always worried if I smell. I remember thinking this was probably why I was forcibly removed.

While I am not a child being controlled or abused anymore, there are still times when I see the impact of their damage appear in my life now.

Of the six or seven short-term placements I had, a few stand out as being positive, while the rest form one sensation of anxiety and fear in my memories. One of the better ones I remember was with a queer couple, Greg and Peter. Greg and Peter were some of the nicest people I ever met.

The reason they stick out as being good ones is simply because they did not try to manipulate, abuse or mistreat me or my family. Greg, Peter and their biological daughter didn't make me feel like I was just a foster kid. They may have made me feel as if I was just at my uncles' home.

Greg and Peter both worked in the creative space and were two genuine, loving people. They spoke so highly of my culture and allowed me to speak of my parents' love. They welcomed this with so much warmth.

But despite feeling comfortable with Greg and Peter, feeling somewhat safe for the first time since being taken, I wasn't allowed to stay with them long. I remember hearing that it wasn't considered 'appropriate' for me, as a young girl, to witness their homosexuality.

Greg and Peter wanted to keep me, I remember that – and not keep me so I wouldn't return to my family, or to act as a barrier between returning home, but keep me because we all got along. But they had been told I would be placed with an Aboriginal family, and they thought it was right to do that. I respect that so much about them. I remember them being very respectful of my culture and wanting to do the right thing.

But the underlying reason for my removal from them was homophobia. They didn't know this, but I did, because I remember the case worker talking to me about how wrong it was. Again, as a kid, I was so confused because I genuinely had a place of safety with them, but they were discriminated against – and again, we all were punished.

When I was taken from Greg and Peter, I thought it was to be placed with an Aboriginal family like they had been told. I won't lie – I was pretty excited. I thought maybe it was Pop or my aunty. I had relatives trying to take on my care and fight for me. Even though my own mother was capable of caring for me, and still had custody of Joseph, they didn't even consider placing me with her. Dad had even completed all the programs and tasks they put to him.

They automatically deemed my mum unacceptable and assumed that she could not meet my needs. They again, throughout the whole process, used my mother's illness as a tool to keep me in a system that didn't know how to love me.

All the time this was happening, the system was watching me and my parents, including having strangers observe the supervised visits I had with Mum and Dad.

I got to read a six-page report from one of these observations as an adult, and the way it was written was so incredibly detached from any understanding of Black families and how community works in our culture.

The only truthful thing I remember being written in that document was along the lines of 'Joseph's really protective of his little sister – he won't let her go in the water without always watching her and making sure she's okay.' Joseph, as my older brother, was always protective of me and always looking out for me.

But instead of that being seen as a strength of our sibling relationship (indeed, something I think white children with younger siblings would be commended for), it was seen as Joseph being saddled with parenting responsibilities and just more evidence of neglect.

But Joseph was never under pressure to parent me. He just knew to look out for his younger sister. It was no different to having to hold hands with your buddy when you're in primary school or being paired with a student from an older year level to help you out if you get lost in your first days at school.

It felt like everything I or my family did was automatically seen through this negative lens.

I've always felt the presence of surveillance.

I felt surveillance in our community when I saw the state coming to do unexpected house checks and welfare checks.

I felt the surveillance when I was in school, and if I had dirty clothes I'd be so terrified that they were going to put a report in on my family of neglect.

I felt surveillance even during my advocacy when I was older. To this day, I'm always cautious of media.

I feel the weight of surveillance, of knowing that the government still has all of these documents and information on me, but they don't have my side of the story – and I'm still waiting to receive records of my time in the system that I requested so long ago.

My parents felt surveillance too, and I can't imagine the hurt and humiliation of having to be watched by strangers while they spent time with their own child, who they loved and cared for. I read that report and wonder why, instead of taking me away from them, they hadn't tried to help my parents – given what they observed was a young girl desperate to be with her parents and siblings.

As I've mentioned, after I was taken, my dad used to come down to the school and visit me through the fence at lunchtime. Aunty Leanne understood how important it was for me to be connected to my family and we considered her part of our family for her support.

There was another unexpected ray of hope in one of my case workers. Despite being moved from short-term placement to short-term placement and being told they wanted to find me an Aboriginal home, I instead went to a home that was abusive and harmful in a number of ways.

Although I told my case workers and begged to be taken out of this place, nothing happened for a long time. Opportunities to speak to my case workers were limited, because they only appeared when I had a contact visit with my parents, for surveillance purposes. Until one day, I had this case worker who was not like the others. I knew straight away that she was on my side. She picked me up from school and took me to see my mum and dad. Mum always knew when something wasn't right, and she could tell straight away that I was hurting.

'Bubba, what's going on? Something's wrong,' she said.

Everything was wrong, but I didn't want to say that – I wanted to enjoy the two hours I got in a month with my family. I was terrified, but I was also a kid and I didn't know how to manage it all.

Mum said, 'Bub, I know you aren't feeling safe.'

The case worker was paying attention. 'What do you think is up?' she asked Mum.

I finally managed to muster up my courage. I told Mum that the people at this foster placement hit me. I said that I was sore, and my eye hurt.

My mum immediately looked at the case worker. 'You need to make sure Vanessa is taken away from this place, and she needs to go to the doctor for her eye.' The case worker assured Mum this would happen.

After visits with my family, my common response was to sleep. I would just disassociate with sleeping to block out the pain of leaving my mum and dad.

This was always the hardest part. I just wanted to go home … my real home.

I remember being tired driving back to the foster home. When we got there, my case worker spoke to the foster carer. Immediately, the foster carer dragged me into the apartment and told me to go to the back.

The case worker wasn't letting it go, though. 'You need to take Vanessa to the doctor straight away for her eye,' she said.

To that, the foster carer simply sneered, 'I'll do what I want to do.'

As she went to slam the door in my case worker's face, I saw her foot stop the door ... she pushed it back open and slapped the foster carer across the face.

It was an extreme reaction, and I don't condone violence in any form – but I was also aware that this was the only person who had stood up for me since I'd been taken from my home.

She listened to my mum, she listened to me. She knew how unsafe I felt and how I wanted the abuse to stop. I wish I could find her and tell her, 'Thank you.'

I never saw that case worker again.

I was faced with another one a few days after and taken out of that bad foster placement.

The cycle continued for multiple more placements before I was finally placed in what would be my last foster care arrangement, where I stayed until I was eighteen and aged out of the system.

Removal from kinship and country is correlated with crossover into the juvenile and criminal justice systems for many First Nations children in out-of-home care. The disproportionate criminalisation and imprisonment of First Nations people is one of the defining features of Australian criminal justice systems and adds additional layers to the trauma of the ongoing effects of colonisation, dispossession from land, the Stolen Generations and centuries of systemic and structural violence.

In Australia and globally there is an alarming increase in families being reported to statutory child protection services during pregnancy and following birth. There remains a crisis where infants are at a high risk of forcible removal. This, again, disproportionately targets First Nations children and families. The thing about First Nations women and children here in Australia is that they find themselves at the ongoing intersections of state violence.

What are meant to be moments of joy, love and excitement can lead very quickly to darkness. Not because of the parent, but simply because of state systems, reporting processes, and often the way domestic and family violence is assessed. There remains a greater risk of child statutory intervention and harm, such as a removal, than of support being provided for parent–survivor and child. This is a reminder that often the pipeline of harm is present from birth, progressing through statutory child removal to the criminal justice system.

With the increase in child removal, we are also starting to see a drastic rise in birth removals through the process of birth alerts occurring in the last few years. This is when reports are made alerting systems such as the department that a baby has been born and that potential care, protection and/or surveillance is needed. This is a harmful process that often works on prediction and bias.

For example, a health practitioner may predict that you cannot raise or care for your child (even though this child is a newborn) by using indicators often associated with poverty and marginalisation, and their own bias. The birth alert can be the start of a mother's worst nightmare. Once the department is alerted, the harm begins. What do we do when the same places that are meant to be for our safety and protection – hospitals and health settings – are actually perpetrators?

I'm discussing infant removal because it has a significant impact on the family policing system. Quite often, people love the idea of adopting, fostering or 'saving' a First Nations child. This discourse has long existed within Australia's historical framework, of wanting to come in and falsely protect the lives of First Nations people. However, what we know is that this idea of protectionism is in fact an act of forcing our assimilation and disrupting our family systems of community and kinship. Often, when our babies are removed, we see the dismissal of identity and cultural protocols being denied.

While at times this may be well-intentioned, it does not ensure the cultural safety and sovereignty of our children. In fact, birth removals are dangerous acts of violence, because through paternalism we see the way newborn babies are often rushed into long-term orders, facing the risk of adoption. Parents who have just given birth are now dealing with their nightmare. While physically and emotionally trying to recover from the actual birth, they have been met with a removal of their baby. This makes it extremely difficult for the child to connect back to their country and community, and the prospects for restoration are incredibly difficult.

Any stage of child removal is incredibly painful for any parent. But imagine that. Imagine holding your newborn, going through magic and back, and having your baby taken.

That is the reality.

That is Australia.

The risk of removal for First Nations babies is significantly disproportionate compared to the broader population, and this has a flow-on effect on First Nations women accessing the healthcare they need during pregnancy and childbirth.

In 2018, I wrote in my thesis for my social work honours that the adoption of our children is a form of permanent separation and denial of cultural birth rights, self-determination and family autonomy. I discussed the implications of intergenerational trauma and the impact of forced adoptions and infancy removal.

My thesis focused on the censoring of First Nations community-controlled organisations and the silencing of their voices. In particular, I explored amendments of the New South Wales *Adoption Act* that removed the need for parental consent in the process of adoption.

Yes, you read that correctly. Children in New South Wales can be adopted without parental consent.

The removal of parental consent disproportionately targets First Nations children and places the power in the hands of the court. The ultimate discretion lies with the judge and the evidence provided. One of the objectives shared by Pru Goward, Minister for Family and Community Services at the time, was that children deserve to feel a sense of belonging – ultimately implying that Indigenous families and communities cannot provide this, but forced adoption can.

Under this amendment to the Act, the Supreme Court may dispense with consent of any person other than the child if the court is satisfied that the child has established a stable relationship with the authorised carer, and the adoption of the child by the authorised carer will promote the child's interests and welfare. It was further stated by then-Premier of New South Wales Gladys Berejiklian that the changes would be a 'relief for foster carers'.

This amendment is a complete failure of the rights of parents and the objective of 'child protection' in ensuring that families are supported. The prioritisation of foster carers having 'relief' over families getting support is shameful. Many community members still today feel completely rejected, and too many of our children are adopted out, losing culture, identity and access to their birth rights.

It is crucial to acknowledge the harm caused by forced adoption, particularly for First Nations children. It is essential to recognise that if a parent is resisting adoption and not providing consent, their rights must also be upheld. Forcing adoption is a distressing repetition of historical practices. Although there are specific protocols when it comes to First Nations children, my experience in the field suggests that they often aren't followed. As a result, the rights and interests of children and families are dehumanised throughout the process.

When a state system is pitted against community members and families who lack access to legal services and effective representation, it becomes highly challenging for the family and child involved in foster care to have a successful outcome. This power imbalance can further perpetuate injustices and make it difficult for families to navigate the child protection system.

I remember as a kid watching the court process play out. I remember seeing my mum break down after every court session. My parents didn't have money for good lawyers; we used our local legal service, which, upon reflection, I truly feel failed all of us. I remember the big scary doors to enter the courtroom, DOCS on one side, my parents on the other. Even though I was sworn in as a practising lawyer as an adult, it's pretty sad to think I was entering rooms like this as a kid.

I remember my mum would wear makeup, and try to have a fresher, new-looking pair of secondhand shoes on. In my heart, this was Mum trying her absolute best to make the system see her as Mum and not her illness – as the strengths and love of who she was, not what they *thought* she was. Even as a kid, I knew she was trying so hard just to be recognised as a human.

I also saw my dad, who would wear a tie, not his usual South Sydney Rabbitohs jersey or jumper. He'd still have his denim blue jeans and nice shoes on (they were also secondhand), but he would wash them up real good for court.

My parents just wanted to be viewed as people. This broke me, because I could feel how unsafe my parents felt, but I could also feel their strength. They were not giving up on me, but, sadly, legal teams were.

The Aboriginal Legal Service (ALS) in Australia was born out of the tireless activism and advocacy of passionate individuals fighting for the rights of and justice for Indigenous peoples. As a lawyer, my heart goes out to the ALS. I can understand the limitations of the service, underfunded and with other challenges; however, as someone who was represented when just a child, I also see failure.

The ALS was a beacon of hope, a much-needed resource for our communities in the midst of systemic injustices. But despite its important role, limitations still persisted, especially when it came to the representation of First Nations families in the flawed family court system.

The ALS played a crucial role in providing legal support and representation for Aboriginal and Torres Strait Islander individuals and families. It was a vital lifeline for those caught in the web of a legal system that often failed to address the specific needs and challenges faced by our communities.

The ALS fought for fair treatment and sought to protect the rights of First Nations peoples, particularly in cases involving incarceration, and also offered support for family law. However, even with the existence of the ALS, the representation provided to First Nations families in the family court system often falls short. A variety of factors contribute to this insufficiency, leaving families vulnerable and disadvantaged.

For First Nations families, the consequences of insufficient representation in the Family Court system are devastating. Children are torn away from their families and communities, and they lose connection to their culture, language and identity. The repercussions are felt for generations, perpetuating the cycle of trauma and cultural disconnection.

As a young child, I witnessed my family's journey through the daunting process of accessing the ALS and navigating the family court system. The image of those imposing courtroom doors stands vividly in my memory, a symbol of the struggles and injustices that awaited us.

I remember being a kid and seeing my parents attempt to wear their best outfits to try to fit the environment, but I also remember them feeling shame because they were up against a violent department.

I am not writing to diminish the ALS by any means; however, as a child who went through this system, and saw the way it worked and failed, I think we must see ALS provided with adequate long-term support, cultural safety and advocacy to keep our families together.

It was a time filled with fear and uncertainty as the department relentlessly sought to find anything that could be used against my family. They seemed determined to tear our family apart, to create a narrative that painted my mum and dad as unsuitable parents, unfit to care for me.

I believe now that this is why my fight to support families runs deep. Because that can be the difference for families: having an advocate or legal representative who backs you.

The unrealistic goals set for parents by the department to demonstrate their fitness and ability to have their children restored into their custody within a two-year period can represent significant challenges.

Often, these goals are accompanied by strict criteria that place a heavy burden on parents rather than providing the necessary support. For instance, if a person requires rehabilitation support or services, the wait times are often lengthy, making it difficult to access timely help, which further delays the restoration process.

The message conveyed to families and communities fighting for their children, seeking support and aiming to break free from the cycle of violence and harm is deeply disheartening. By imposing a specific time limit and demanding parents prove their capabilities within that timeframe while simultaneously creating barriers that hinder their ability to meet those requirements, the system sends a strong signal that their worthiness as parents is in question. This approach fails to acknowledge the complexities and challenges families face and undermines their efforts to be reunified with their children.

As I review my personal case files, it's evident that my parents did everything they could to regain custody of me.

One of the department's requirements was for Dad to attend counselling and address his issues with drinking. He put forth tremendous effort, attending every counselling session except for one. I read through the file myself and discovered that he had missed that one session because he already had a prior appointment, and he had informed the counsellor of this. However, the department used this as evidence to claim that Dad was incapable of raising me, disregarding the consistent attendance in the other sessions.

The department also employed tactics such as abruptly changing visiting days to catch Dad off guard. It was devastating to witness the system placing additional pressure on him, considering his struggles. They were eager to document any perceived failure that they could then use it against him in court.

If our society continues to focus solely on the negatives rather than recognising the strengths of families and communities, we will perpetuate a harmful cycle and set families up for failure.

When I speak about the safest place for an Aboriginal child being in the womb, it's because that is where they cannot be physically torn away from their parents. However, once a child is born, the danger begins, as the system can intercede and police the family. I see the system's abuse, violence and reproductive control inflicted upon First Nations bodies, particularly those of First Nations women.

The Australian health system continues to perpetrate abuse and racism, punishing First Nations children for being born into struggle and poverty, as if it were their parents' fault, deeming them destined for failure. In an attempt to 'fix' this, the system removes them from their families. Public health remains a violent sphere where the state commits crimes in various ways, and although health professionals may argue that they're acting in the best interests of these children, they often cause greater harm.

I have spent time with First Nations mothers who have had their children taken away from them, as well as mothers who are now grandmothers fighting to reunite with their grandchildren. It has become clear that what is referred to as 'child protection' is truly the opposite. The system, which was supposed to respond and protect, consistently fails to do so.

I often find myself reflecting on my mother and the fear she experienced when she discovered she was pregnant again; her premonition that her child would once again be taken from her. As the mother of my own daughter, I am now in a similar position, and I struggle deeply when I contemplate the pain that the department's decisions inflicted upon her.

I understand the immense love I have for my daughter, just as my mother loved me. Our connection is undeniable.

No-one, except other survivors of these systems, will ever fully understand my experience.

The fear still lingers within me at times.

LOVE AND BELONGING

T HE NIGHT I WAS STOLEN, everything changed. I was taken from my home, my family, my life. And the hardest part is this: when they took me, my dad fell into an even deeper depression. His whole world had just been ripped apart, shattered into a million pieces. And then he tried everything to get me back. It breaks me. To this day, I can remember feeling everything my father endured during these moments, watching him break.

What the department doesn't speak about is the impact this has on parents and those left in the community when they rip a child away. Don't take this as me saying that we leave kids in dangerous situations – absolutely not. But I mean this: there is a serious separation when it comes to best interests of children. When these so-called 'experts' (often known as case workers) take a child from their family, parent or the one person they have only known because they have decided they are a danger to that child, they don't for a second think of the needs of the person they are ripping the child from.

Have you ever watched the strongest person you know collapse into thin air, as if their soul is being ripped from their body? The night they stole me, my dad passed me his heart and soul. He sent me protection while neglecting himself in every way.

And as a parent now, what I do know for sure is that if anyone tries to take my child, every part of me will be taken with her. I'll be left with nothing, because she is my everything.

Even while completely broken, my dad followed their orders, desperate to prove that he could be the parent they wanted him to be. They recommended drug and alcohol counselling programs, and he enrolled in every one of them. He showed up faithfully, determined to do whatever it took to bring me home. He missed one session, just one, and they used it against him.

'Mr Roberts has gone to eleven out of the twelve sessions,' they said. 'He's not fit to be a parent.' It was like they were looking for any tiny flaw, any opportunity to tear him down. But no-one ever acknowledged his strengths. No-one ever acknowledged the fact that he went to eleven sessions, that he was fighting with every fibre of his being to reunite our family.

I seriously wonder what kind of world we are creating if this is the response we give to people trying their absolute best to fight for their children. It's a world that values perfection over effort, that judges without mercy, and in the end, it's the children who suffer the most.

They took so much more than just me that night.

At the time I was taken, Joseph and I were technically living together with Dad. It was the three of us, our small family unit clinging to each other for support. Mum was living at Eastgardens by this point, after a house fire.

When I was a little kid, Mum's house caught on fire. Some people say she did it, some say it was a cigarette that never went out, others say it was a neighbour who set it on fire. To this day we do not know what actually caused the fire in the housing commission flat. There was no investigation or anything, from my own memory. We lost everything, and it's why I don't have many photos of Mum or Dad, or of Joseph and me as little kids. The house that burnt down was a three-bedroom apartment just up the road from Dad's, but after this Mum was placed into a one-bedroom apartment. We would be over there all the time as kids, and we would all share a bed – Mum and her two kids.

Living together brought us closer in ways we couldn't have imagined. We laughed together, cried together and held each other up when we thought we couldn't bear the weight of our loss. Mum loved cuddling me to sleep. She would stroke my eyebrows, sing to me and constantly worry whether I was okay or not. My mother and motherhood are truly the most special. And if I am honest, it's while raising my own jarjum that I reflect even more deeply on the love of my mother. I have the joy of being a mother myself, but the way I love, raise and nurture my daughter is from the mothering I was shown, the love I was given. The love that the department never saw, that they only chose to give hate. Three bedrooms or one bedroom, the flat held us together, and while public housing can make you feel incredibly trapped – it's intentionally built like a prison, a small square box – my goodness, being with each other was the greatest act of love for all of us.

Our community was a small one, with its own unique offerings. We had a jail, a local community centre and a cemetery. But we also had something darker, something that lurked in the shadows. Horrifyingly, we had a block of housing dedicated to known child sexual perpetrators in our local area. It was a chilling reminder that danger could be so close, hidden in plain sight. But the reality was there, a haunting presence that could not be ignored. There were dangerous times for me that I was placed in and would not wish for anybody. As a child I was subject to dangerous circumstances, but the circumstances were systemically designed to set us kids up for the harm we faced.

As I look back now, with the wisdom of hindsight, I read the reports and analyse the reasons for my removal. They talk about me playing outside. Playing. When did playing become a crime for kids? It's a question that lingers in my mind, a bitter taste of injustice. But I think what they meant was the danger of this place. And it was dangerous. We lived around danger. But my question is: why have this? Why have such a place that exists in a space where kids play and roam? A place that's our home?

In the midst of the chaos and heartache, it became clear that the true crime did not lie within our family but in the presence of the perpetrators that surrounded us. However, as a Black family, we were the target of the state.

Placing blame on my parents or my family was not the answer. It was the system they had built, the environment they had subjected us to, that wasn't safe. As a parent myself and a professional in this space, I understand the desperation to protect your children, but not at the cost of paternalism or the false idea that the Western way is the only right way. The system failed to understand our surroundings and as a result my father was punished. The system did not choose to hear my voice or interpret my needs.

I often wonder if I should have spoken up. I was terrified.

On the night they stole me, Joseph decided to go stay at Mum's place.

It struck me later: if Mum was not considered a viable option for my care, why didn't they take Joseph too? And if she was considered capable of caring for Joseph, why not place me with her, my own mother? This should have been the pathway taken, with Mum supported.

Dad struggled with the racism he faced in this colony, in this place. He carried the weight of his own experiences of discrimination, exclusion and disempowerment. And it was hard, so hard.

The generational trauma we experienced had a profound impact on our family.

It was a trauma that stemmed from the generational removal and cultural erasure faced by First Nations families like ours. My nana May Brown was a survivor of the dark legacy of slavery on Cubbawee Mission. She was forcibly taken, a victim of child removal, generational removal and cultural removal. When I was stolen, the department was following in the footsteps of this historical injustice. It wasn't just about removing children. It was about erasing our culture, our identity, our very essence.

As I grapple with the pain of separation, I can't help but wonder what kind of world we're creating. A world where cultural diversity is brushed aside, where Indigenous voices are silenced and disregarded. A world that values assimilation over preservation, a world that perpetuates the false notion that there is only one 'right' way to live.

Love is inherent in the collective fight for justice and liberation within my community. It flows through the veins of my brothers, my sisters, my siblings, my kin and our entire community. Love is the foundation on which we build our resistance and resilience. It is the seeds that we plant and nurture, knowing that they will grow and flourish for generations to come. First Nations love is transformative, creating a sense of belonging and unity that cannot be replicated. It is a force that drives us forward, reminding us of our strength, our culture and our shared identity. If you get to be loved by a First Nations person, hold that close – it's a different type of love – of healing, connection and liberation. It's a force where you get to be invited to knowing just a little of the two-hundred-and-fifty-plus years of who we are and who we always will be. Often when you are loved with or by a First Nations person, you get to be loved by all we come from. Our ancestors, our people.

Facing grief is a journey. It's hard, especially within the context of the family policing system, which perpetuates loss and separation. Grief does not always need to be personal, though, or complex. Sometimes it's clear as day in front of our eyes. The family policing system forces us to grieve the living, to mourn the disconnection from our loved ones, and the loss of our first attachments and connections. Grief can become a constant companion, a shadow that follows us throughout our lives. I experienced grief very young, and while I remain alive, there is also this deep pain of loss in my heart and little body from being taken.

In my own journey of grief, I have learned to redefine my relationship with the spirit world. A wise sister, Marlikka, shared with me the importance of not forgetting to communicate with those who are no longer physically present. She reminded me that our relationships with our ancestors and loved ones transcends the physical realm and that we can still lean on them, speak to them and shower them with love.

Marlikka emphasised the significance of maintaining this connection, as our ancestors reside in our ancestral lands, offering us guidance, safety and solace. She often shares that 'country needs company'. I hold firm in the knowledge that Dad has returned home to Bundjalung country, to a place where he is at peace and protected. I was only twenty years old, soon to be twenty-one, when I climbed through his housing commission window, and there I found my dad, laying on the floor, gone. Physically there but gone.

Navigating a world filled with fear and challenges is a reality that many First Nations individuals and communities face. I actually think we all face it, but it's much more present for my people. The constant needing to be cautious, reflecting on what one is saying, doing and being. I mean, simply existing is a threat to this place as a Blackfulla. However, with love, a sense of belonging and a supportive community, we find strength and assurance.

My dear sister Nayuka, a proud Gunai/Kurnai, Wiradjuri and Yorta Yorta person, has been a guiding presence in my life. During a visit to Narrm (Melbourne) after my dad had died, Nayuka and I took a moment to have a coffee and a walk. In our conversation, they asked if Dad had come to visit. To non-Indigenous people, this might seem unfathomable. What does it mean to have the dead visit? But for us, spiritual visitors are a part of our reality. In fact, they are very physical in their presence, or their smell, or touch. Our ancestors and loved ones often visit us, providing comfort and reassurance in our lives.

I vividly recall my dad visiting me after he passed on. He often stared and didn't speak too much. In another memory I recall Mum sitting at the end of my bed. My dad continues to visit me often, and my mum, well she is always around my daughter, Waitui.

You see, for my people, we never really die – we transform, we dream, we move on. As Indigenous people, historically we have always grieved collectively and with others. We have been held so deeply with care and community; just as country needs company, death often keeps us company when we tune into it.

I have lost so many people that I have had no choice but to change my relationship with death. But when there is an injustice to a death, a crime by the system on my people, this is when death is complicated, because the violence of the colony has failed to allow us to do our grieving properly, because attached to this, is so much pain, time on inquests, advocating for basic truth to be prevailed.

Sadly, now with death, we don't get to grieve in a way we should be able to. We struggle deeply. To pay for costs of funerals, to demand justice, to have our people together because displacement has done such a horrific job at ensuring the fight to come together is harder. While my people today struggle to fund funerals, traditionally this would have been done with no costs. The harm in money, death and pain continues.

Another visitor is an uncle. This uncle is a wise Yuin elder. When my daughter Waitui was just a newborn, Uncle came to her cot and drew a wave on a piece of bark. Sadly, Uncle had recently passed away. My daughter's name means 'chief' and 'ocean', and Uncle also shared a deep love for the whales, animals and the ocean. The whale is a big part of our song lines, and connects through the stories up north, through to Tasmania, Melbourne and Western Australia, crossing the waters.

The relationships of the spiritual world are powerful, and they work in incredible ways. Through these spiritual encounters, I have learned valuable lessons and experienced a profound connection with the wisdom and guidance of my ancestors.

Aunty Calita and Uncle Dean, who resided in La Perouse for a significant period, played a crucial role in my healing journey. They cared for the community without expecting anything in return – simply respect for each other, for land, for spirit. When I ran away from the system, they provided immense support and did extensive healing work with me. They imparted invaluable knowledge and shared stories with me, but I am aware that there is so much more that I have yet to learn.

An elder's wisdom extends far beyond this earthly realm, demonstrating the immense power of kinship and love in fostering a sense of belonging. That is who my people are. We take people in, we love them, we nurture them. Isn't it sad that there is a whole system dedicated to taking us away from our families, but yet, my people are caretakers, opening up our homes, supporting communities and always showing up.

When I was taken from my parents, I witnessed a piece of them die inside. As a mother myself, I understand the profound pain that would come from something or someone coming between me and my child.

In the realm of love, belonging, grief and loss, I have learned to find love within my grief. I have found solace in communicating with the ancestors and building my relationships with them. This doesn't mean that I embrace death, but it means that I have had to cultivate a deeper spiritual practice to cope with my loss.

I have experienced the loss of both my parents. My father died just before my twenty-first birthday, and my mother took her own life on the night of my father's funeral. Without delving into the legal intricacies, I can say that her suicide was a result of the system's failure to provide her with the help she so desperately needed.

I guess I should reword this: my mother didn't take her life; she was failed by those who were meant to assist her and protect her life – just as their attempts to protect and care for me resulted in stress, worry and ultimate failure.

I remember like it was just yesterday, the calling for help, the begging for someone to know what to do, for answers. While deeply grieving and having just buried my dad, I was met with the greatest nightmare I ever faced — a phone call for help that resulted in me holding another funeral two weeks later.

I pleaded for help, spending over three-and-a-half hours on the phone with the mental health emergency team, desperately trying to get someone to assist my mother. During this time, I knew in my gut that something bad was about to happen. I sat by the Elphinstone Road housing flats in Coogee after checking on my mum after leaving Dad's sorry business early, and I knew she was not okay. I made attempts to reach dear friends and family regarding my mum's welfare, I expressed that 'something is not right'. I was with two other friends, who sat beside me as I pleaded for help. But nobody came.

The mental health emergency team dismissed my concerns. I spoke with agencies who position themselves as places to call in circumstances like the one my mum and I were in. Instead they began claiming that they had worked with First Nations people before and knew what was best. My mum wasn't Indigenous. The assumption that she was, and the fatal results of that assumption, shows both the level of ignorance on behalf of those taking the call and, yet again, the lack of care these systems have for Indigenous bodies.

The saddest part is my mum managed her illness so well — she had regular check-ups, the medication she was on required regular blood tests, and all this information would have been available when they looked up my mum's details. Instead of taking her life seriously when it needed to be, they dismissed her. They dismissed me. They failed all of us. Again.

To this day, the pain of losing my mother weighs heavily on me. Mum instilled in me the importance of health, wellbeing and education. She always wanted the best for our family. Although we were financially disadvantaged, our love and sense of belonging remained our greatest wealth. We took care of one another, nurtured our connection with nature and made sure our community was okay. Now that my parents are no longer with me physically, I hold tightly to the nights Mum comes and sleeps with me. Or when I see her checking on Waitui. My dad is often around my partner, Ellia, also.

In death, nobody really dies. Death can be weird. All things. Every emotion. What does this world hold beyond the physical realm? How do we navigate life when our anchors are no longer physically present? What does it mean when visitors come in the night to say hello, sit at the end of my bed or hold my hand when I'm scared, even though they can only be felt in spirit? What does it mean when my daughter is crying and suddenly she looks over my shoulder and smiles? What does it mean when I see her in the middle of the night, laughing and looking up, as if engaged in a joyful conversation? I know these are the spirits of our ancestors visiting her. I know it's my mum, dad, nan, pop, uncle, friends, family.

I know loss too well.

I am heartbroken that my daughter cannot be physically present with my parents.

But I am certain that they are here with us, strong and ever present.

Love and belonging require us to be open to these conversations, to create spaces for healing and sharing, and to allow ourselves to break as long as we remain safe.

As Indigenous people, these conversations are crucial because death is an ever-present shadow in our lives. We must be open with each other, holding one another and loving one another.

I firmly believe that our people have always possessed the knowledge and practices of communal care. It is within the fabric of who we are. Responsibility for the land, for each other and for our children has always fallen upon us.

We are not to blame for the injustices and deaths that have plagued our communities. It is deeply hurtful to constantly hear narratives suggesting that we are incapable of raising our own children or taking responsibility for what works within our communities. If those in positions of authority who can genuinely make change actually care about the lives of my people, they must first remove the intrusive interventions of the state and grant Indigenous communities autonomy, choice and love. The notion that we are not capable is inherently racist and continues to cause harm.

Audre Lorde once powerfully stated: 'I am not free while any woman is unfree, even when her shackles are very different from my own.' Now that I have found personal freedom within the confines of a world that still targets Indigenous communities,

I see my work as giving back. That is my mission. Free all our children and young. Free my people, with the people.

I grew up in a community where failure seemed to be the expected outcome for many of us. As I mentioned before, we grew up with a jail next door, a local community centre that provided my Vegemite and cheese sandwiches and the free milk and milo that I loved, and sadly, just down the road, a cemetery.

I loved my local community centre. Julie who ran it continued to show up for so many. She often had a foul mouth, but if you needed something she had your back. I would go there after school for a sandwich and a milo, and she would always make extra for me. This place meant so much to so many. Today it has sadly changed hands and the way it works. I wish my community still had a place to go to, but if I am honest even with these places, we are still harmed.

Funerals were more common than celebrations. This was the reality of living in a community plagued by constant surveillance and policing designed to isolate us. Systemic violence was a daily occurrence, with police abusing their power against children and community members. The case workers would come all well dressed, appearing to be 'better' than all of us, in preparation to steal children, and while I witnessed these events, nothing could prepare me for the night they would come and steal me.

In my childhood, I saw more police officers than schoolteachers. They were a constant presence, policing our communities and instilling fear within us. This was the norm, and we always had to act with caution. As children, we stuck together, keeping watch for each other, ensuring someone always had their eyes and ears on the police. We didn't have phones to document their abuses back then, but today, even when we witness instances of police violence, accountability seems to elude us, and the value placed on our lives is minimal.

My father remained in our family housing commission flat until his last breath. At just twenty years old, I found myself breaking into our old flat, the one we lived in before I was taken. I shattered a window to gain entry, only to find my father laying on the floor. It was a moment of sheer agony, one that will forever be etched in my memory.

I often have flashbacks to that moment when I climbed in because my older brother Joseph was too scared to. I smashed the window, landed on the kitchen sink and jumped down. I walked just around the corner, and there was Dad – my whole world changed once again. My best friend, gone. When I reflect on that place, all I see is pain. I feel the weight of that pain, the hurt, the anger. I am angry that I was taken from those walls at the age of ten-and-a-half, and then, at twenty, my father was taken from me. It happened on the October long weekend, the same weekend as our Koori Knockout.

The Koori Knockout is an annual event that is like Black Christmas, where Aboriginal communities from all over New South Wales come together to watch football. It's a weekend of community showcasing our talents and strengths. My dad loved football, especially the Koori Knockout. He grew up playing and was part of the Redfern Rovers and Redfern All Blacks teams. He played alongside the respected Uncle Shane, and until his last breath he reminisced about his memories of winning the grand final, sprinting to secure the winning try as he played on the wing.

The morning I found my dad was the morning I was supposed to pick him up and take him to the Koori Knockout so he could watch the community play. But we never made it to the Knockout. My father didn't even make it through the living room. I found him there, on the floor … gone.

These same walls, where my world was once broken and shattered, also held my father's suffering. The place I had been stolen from, the housing flats in Bilga, was the same flat where I found my dad dead. I lay next to him, promising to care for Joseph and assuring Dad that everything would be okay. He could finally find rest from this harmful world.

The torment and racism that my father endured in this colony seemed to drain the years from his life. A proud Bundjalung man, my father was softly spoken and avoided conflict. He was the kind of person anyone could hold a conversation with. He fixed things and was known as the handyman in our housing complex. Every other day, someone had something Dad could assist with.

He loved walking, and you could find him with his two kids by his side, walking everywhere. Although he loved cars, he had lost his licence due to numerous fines and demerit points.

Dad often relied on the bus and even the good old 'Foot Falcon' (which refers to walking instead of driving a car). He had a lot of love and respect for bus drivers, always striking up conversations or saying something positive. On weeks when we didn't have money, bus drivers who knew my dad would let us on for free.

In our housing complex, there was always something for my dad to do. During council pick-up weeks, he would strategically walk around with a trolley and collect broken items, such as washing machines, old TVs or couches. He would fix them and offer them to someone in the community who might need them, often prioritising mothers with children.

Did my dad have demons? Of course. But, as a child, I didn't fully see or understand them. As an adult, I reflect on my dad and recognise that he did the best he could. It didn't have to mean taking his daughter away from him and tearing us apart. It could have meant getting him the help he deserved. You see, my dad wasn't born with these demons. The demons reside in the blood of a society that refuses to support, opting for punitive measures instead.

Intergenerational trauma is often spoken about in our community. It's the concept of pain and trauma being passed on when left unsupported and unhealed. My great-grandparents were slaves to a system designed to fail them. For more than half his life, my father wasn't even considered a human or citizen on his own land. He was constantly targeted by the police, and like me, he lost his mother when he was just twenty-one.

Though he wasn't perfect, the way we respond to our trauma differs. My father needed help, deeper love. Instead, he was met with the shattering violence of the system. Yet, my dad remained a gentle soul, and he, along with my mum, were my best friends. They taught me everything I needed to know.

About three weeks before I found my dad lifeless, he urged me to promise that if anything happened to my brother, I would call an ambulance instead of the police. My father really took care of Joseph, as did Mum. When Joseph was twelve years old he was diagnosed with schizophrenia, but he was never supported holistically by the community support team. I think Dad knew in his gut something was about to happen to him, and to be honest, my father was a stubborn Black man, so even if he was diagnosed with something, typical Blackfulla, he would not tell anybody, and the last thing Dad ever wanted was to worry me. So he said, 'The police will shoot first before asking any questions.' And he wasn't wrong. As children, my dad taught us to remain silent when encountering a police officer, educating us on the importance of never turning our backs or running. Just remain silent.

How many non-Indigenous parents contemplate these teachings? How many white families have to consider when to educate their children about the law and the reality of being subjected to policing? I never understood why this education began so early for us. Growing up in our community, we knew that the police would shoot. Now, as an adult, I know that even when you comply and follow protocols, as a First Nations person, the chances of death or harm increase when taken into custody or in the presence of police. I was only ten-and-a-half, after all, when they placed my hands behind my back and ripped me from my dad.

Dad knew these dangers firsthand. He shared a story with me about his time in lockup with other Koori boys from Redfern and other places. A policeman mocked and abused my father, sticking his fingers up his nose and calling him racial slurs. Dad shared this story when I was nineteen years old. This is what state-sanctioned violence does – it systematically kills and impacts lives without respite.

Love and belonging require transformative justice and safe spaces. We find belonging in our place and community, where healing and warmth grow strong. Love and belonging allow us to speak our truths, sharing the struggles we face and allowing them to be nurtured in safety.

When I was a child, during the stolen years when time was taken away from me, I did not see love or belonging. However, my parents had already imprinted in my being the essence of love and belonging. I held on to this, I held on to it so close. It ultimately made me the person I am today. Not the system, but the love imprinted from when I was child, those first ten years.

To anyone impacted by state-sanctioned forcible removals and harm, my advice is this: you *do* belong, you *are* loved. I know it's challenging to believe, especially in places where you've been denied this love and belonging. But I promise you, you are loved, and your strength and healing come from a lineage that has existed since the first sunrise and will continue until the last.

THE STATE

IS NOW

YOUR PARENT

ONCE THE DECISION HAD BEEN made that I would remain in the minister's care until I was eighteen, it felt like suddenly everyone was doing everything they could to keep me away from my family and from any connections to my culture or Indigeneity. First, I was taken out of the primary school I had been attending, even though I only had one more year to go.

The family I was placed with was a white family, with two children of their own. They had a daughter, who was about ten years older than me, and a son, also much older then me. I actually got along well with both siblings, who had a fraught relationship with their parents, as I was about to find out. The foster carers, let's call them Jim and Sarah, were working class. They ran a landscaping and cleaning business, and it felt like they were always just trying to get more money. My impression was that the only reason they were foster carers was for the allowance, and whenever a chance came up for an emergency placement, to host a foreign student for school or something like that, if there was money involved, Jim and Sarah would put their hands up.

I felt like Sarah ultimately had good intentions, or maybe back when she had originally agreed to be a foster carer it was for positive reasons. But it never felt like they really cared for me the entire time I was there. Jim sort of ran the household, and I could see that there wasn't really a sense of love or connection in the family. Not with their own kids, and definitely not with me. I remember I'd feel so strange about Christmas time and so strange about holidays because those times that you would typically connect as a family just ... weren't the same.

From the first days I was with them, I knew this was not going to be a safe or welcoming environment for me, especially culturally. I was constantly told to hide my Aboriginality, to not tell people I was Aboriginal and to say no to a counsellor or any other external support.

They monitored what I ate at all times because, as they told me, they thought I would get 'fat' – and that was something they wanted to avoid. And when I was in Year 7, or Year 8, they tried to force me to start taking the contraceptive pill, because they didn't want me to get pregnant. So many assumptions and stereotypes were at play about what I would do, what I was at risk of, as an Aboriginal girl in the system.

Thankfully, despite their best efforts to keep me away from my parents, my mum continued to be my biggest advocate, especially for my education. I know that Mum is the reason I finished Year 12 and why I went to university, because every time I saw her she would remind me that if I got a degree, I could do better than the system I was in.

When I was in Year 10, I was working for the National Centre of Indigenous Excellence, and through them I found out about a program called the Indigenous Youth Leadership Program. I decided to apply, and I was excited when I got in.

As part of the program, I travelled to Melbourne for a week of activities. I was so excited to be with other mob again. It was something I had been yearning for in my heart.

The program started at the National Centre of Indigenous Excellence, and we did a couple of days of future planning. One activity was to design what a better future looks like. I drew a house, and it had layers to it. Some would have called it an organisation, or perhaps a community or village, but to me it was a huge home.

It had three layers inside. At the bottom was a welcoming space, with studios and arts spaces, and the middle had a library and places to access resources and education. And then at the top, I drew these beds and showers where people could stay if they had nowhere to go. I called it: 'Treaty for one, treaty for more, treaty for all.'

Australia is one of the few Commonwealth countries that does not have a treaty with its Indigenous people. I have been fortunate to spend time with elders and community members where discussions about treaty have been central, emphasising the concept as a way for both parties to meet halfway. I think this is where my treaty vision stemmed from as a young person.

Being someone working in the legal field, I am aware that many treaties worldwide with Indigenous peoples are not honoured. However, I strongly believe in advocating for a treaty here. Recognising our sovereignty in this land, it is crucial to establish an agreement through fair negotiations, with enforceable obligations, that empower my people to have true authority and decision-making power over our lands, affairs and futures. Having these conversations with mob was empowering.

When I came back to the foster home, I was even more firmly resolved to get out of there. I was fifteen or sixteen at the time, and I knew I only had a few more years before I could do what I wanted to do. I saved up, and I bought a Toyota Corolla called Bluebird.

When I turned eighteen, I realised that my body was no longer a commodity for the state, so I ran. I ran to my country, Bundjalung, for the first time. It was a physical return to the place my dad and I often talked about, where Pop Collin used to drive trucks through. It was a place of connection and belonging.

You can rock up to literally any mob with nothing, with absolutely nothing, and you'll be taken in. There's nothing more safe than an aunty saying, 'Welcome home, bub,' or,

'Come in, bub. There's a feed here.' And I say that to any mob, any mob that may have been taken or feel worried or scared or they're disconnected or don't have a place to go. It makes me cry. But there is always someone there for you and always home and an aunty or an uncle or a sibling. I found that on country, and it gave me the healing I needed.

But when I returned to Gadigal to complete my studies, I couldn't go back to the foster system. I was scared to ask my own parents if I could live with them. I was incredibly confused. I had lost where I belonged.

That's what the system does. The system told me that my parents didn't want me, that they couldn't take care of me because of my mum's mental illness and my dad's inability. I felt like a burden, and my heart did not want to add to the burden.

I had a place at the University of New South Wales, but without somewhere to live, I didn't know how I was going to make it through university. I was originally enrolled in social work and criminology, and I found the latter quite boring, that it was missing a lot of the point and the work that mattered to me.

I then moved to social work and journalism, because at one point in time I wanted to be a sports reporter. I loved the idea of watching sporting events and commentating on them. I did my work placement in high school at Channel 9 in Artarmon, where I shadowed and worked with sports reporters. I thought this was so fun as a young person.

One day, I was at university, not able to sit still and not happy with the second part of my degree. I spoke to a friend and said, 'Hey, I want to study law.' I then met with someone who would become one of the closest people in my world, who I respect, admire and love deeply. We shared a coffee and a yarn and they promised to always be there – not just for my law degree, but also for the crazy world that often comes with challenges, and of course blessings too. Every single step of the way, this person was by my side, became my family. I don't take this lightly.

When you're a young person who grew up in the system, you learn to read people, to see who is genuine, who isn't. You take the people who choose you to be part of their lives and those who you choose to allow into yours very seriously. You protect each other, you hold each other to account and, no matter what, you remember the foundation of love.

This person's spirit was genuine. They told me that I would need to get my mark to a distinction average to be eligible for an internal transfer, so I focused really hard on my degree, got my marks up and transferred to law.

I started my degree without knowing where to go or where I was going to live. I had my car, a few things and a sister who was on her way to Gadigal. When I had nowhere to stay, but had made some connections with the mob, a sister named Bridget let me stay on her floor. Bridget was studying law and she showed up for me, never asking for anything in return. She is one of the strongest and most loving Black women I've known, someone who had my back.

Shania, a Wakka Wakka woman from Rocky, was also starting her degree. We had plans to get an apartment together and figure things out. But a few months passed, and even though we didn't have the apartment, we held on to the trust that something would work out. And it did.

That's when I applied for a Gamarada Scholarship, a program that provided accommodation for students. I received a phone call about my scholarship application for accommodation support. I had missed the call out of nervousness but, when I listened to the voicemail, I learned I had been invited for an interview. I went to the interview and, after sharing my need for a place, they offered me a scholarship to stay at Shalom College. But I couldn't accept it without mentioning Shania and how incredible she was. In the end, they offered both of us scholarships. I was not going to leave my sister hanging.

This was a turning point for me. It provided stability and guaranteed accommodation as I started my journey. Growing up in the state's family policing system, I never knew if I would have stability or not. The system always looked for what wasn't working and promised to make it better. Every day, I wondered where I would be next, what conditions I would face and if I would ever get to go back home to my parents. But for the first time, I had some control and stability in my life, thanks to the scholarship. It wasn't based on conditions, just to thrive and work towards my education. I now understand why Mum instilled in me the importance of getting an education, because it really is a step towards freedom and it's a fundamental right for all.

Hilton Immerman, who interviewed me for the scholarship and who offered us the opportunity, didn't have to do it, but he did. I wonder if he knew he was offering more than just a room; he was offering stability and a sense of control. That moment was liberating, knowing that I had some say in my own life. As soon as I found out I was accepted into Shalom College, I went there, grateful for a place to call home.

I will be honest with you, so many foster kids struggle with the world. After being in a system that is hard enough, sorting out housing and income, feeling safe and getting access to resources are all incredibly hard. Somehow, something was looking out for me, and I am not thrilled at the fact that someone stepped up to give me an opportunity – but I am thankful, because the pathway could have been different. Having this place as my home, in a time of deep confusion, meant everything. I could do my studies, I could connect with others and I could do this beside my sister. I won't ever take for granted being offered a place that allowed me to choose, instead of a place I was forced to be in.

Shalom was a beautiful Jewish place that allowed me to learn more and connect more.

If you can offer stability in the struggle, that is the greatest gift. We all deserve safety and security.

MOTHERHOOD

AND LOVE

MOTHERHOOD IS A SACRED JOURNEY filled with joy, challenges and endless love. For First Nations mothers, this journey often carries the weight of historical trauma, systemic racism and violence. First Nations women have been unfairly subjected to health racism and the heartbreaking removal of our children.

Hospitals, intended to be safe spaces, have become institutions of separation and loss for First Nations children. However, despite these adversities, First Nations mothers are resilient and determined to raise our children with strength and love.

This chapter explores the experiences, challenges and hopes of First Nations mothers as we navigate motherhood while healing from our own trauma.

As First Nations mothers we bear the scars of historical trauma, alongside our kin, a legacy woven into the fabric of our being born out of Australia's biggest feature of invasion. We also carry the stories of our ancestors, who endured colonisation, forced assimilation and the destruction of our traditional ways of life.

This trauma manifests in various forms, including mental health struggles, addiction and unresolved grief. It becomes an added challenge in this colony, where the violence is so strong.

The wounds of child removal run deep.

One of the most devastating consequences of historical trauma and health racism is the removal of First Nations children from their families. For far too long, First Nations mothers have experienced the anguish of our children being taken away, disrupting the bonds of love and connection. This separation not only fractures families but also perpetuates generational trauma, making it even more challenging for mothers to provide a nurturing environment.

It is often argued that if a mother is struggling with drug addiction while pregnant, she will not be able to parent. The other 'justification' is straight-up racism.

Contrary to their intended purpose as places of healing, hospitals have become institutions of removal for First Nations children.

The stories of First Nations women giving birth only to have their babies taken away without their consent is heartbreaking and infuriating. Instead of supporting mothers and children, hospitals have become a source of great pain and loss.

This phenomenon continues to this day, and the over-representation of First Nations children in child protection systems is a stark reminder of this.

Earlier in this book, I shared the story with you of the fears my parents both had when I was born. These fears carried through when I was pregnant with my own daughter. I couldn't help but feel a sense of fear and apprehension. The stories I had heard, my own lived experiences and the knowledge of historical trauma deeply rooted in my being made the hospital experience daunting.

Hospitals, which are meant to be places of safety and healing, have unfortunately been mired in the mistreatment and removal of First Nations children. The fear of having my child taken away without consent, and losing the precious bond between us, loomed over me. Even as a lawyer with a social work qualification I remained terrified of this.

This fear is not unfounded. It is grounded in the painful truth of the mistreatment and injustices faced by First Nations women within the healthcare system. The hospitals that should have been spaces of trust and support have become sites of pain, loss and the continuation of intergenerational trauma.

With all of this, I knew I had to be prepared. First, I immersed myself in understanding my rights as a patient and a mother. Researching hospital policies and protocols allowed me to advocate for myself and my desires during the birthing process. I sought out information to ensure that my voice would be heard and respected. I also educated my partner and shared that if anything was to happen to me, to not leave the baby.

Equally important was building a support system. I surrounded myself with individuals who understood my concerns and could stand by my side in the hospital setting. Having a trusted family member, which I did, provided me with the extra comfort I needed. Their presence provided emotional support, helped with communication, and ensured that my wishes were honoured.

Acknowledging and addressing my fear was a very real act of empowerment. I wonder if non-Indigenous people or people going through the private system face these fears. I highly doubt it. By taking proactive steps, engaging in open communication and embracing alternative birthing options, I was able to navigate the hospital experience with resilience.

As a First Nations mother, I am determined to protect the bond I share with my daughter, Waitui, and provide her with a nurturing and empowering environment, despite the historical and ongoing trauma that we still see today.

A mother deserves love, support and nourishment. She embodies love itself. When I first held my daughter in my arms, I held on to her tightly, almost instinctively. In that moment, I couldn't help but wonder if this tight grip was driven by a genuine fear or subconscious concern about potential risks and who or what could take her away from me. However, as I gazed into my child's eyes, I saw a love that reached depths I had never known before.

As I reflect deeply on that moment, my heart breaks, knowing that too many mothers experience a similar sense of love, only to have their reality marred by the presence of child protection workers, police and other individuals in positions of power who can remove their children. Being a survivor of the family policing system, I was acutely aware of the serious risk of removal.

I won't deny that I had genuine fears. A few months after giving birth to Waitui, I actually stopped going to therapy. Looking back, I now realise that my decision was fuelled by the fear of my daughter being reported. I immediately responded with surveillance trauma, which is a common fear we carry as survivors due to our history of being watched and the particular circumstances of trauma as children. It wasn't that there was anything to report about me, but this fear had deeply rooted itself within me, causing extreme anxiety during therapy sessions.

Perhaps my therapist sensed some of this fear as well, but I was caught up in overthinking everything. I now understand that my apprehension stemmed from the profound awareness of how it feels to be forcibly separated from family and the risk of interacting with those in a position to report. I never wanted Waitui to experience that pain, and I thought about my therapist doing this. This only speaks to the level of anxiety I carried, and upon reflection, I wish I had been open with my therapist about it. However, a good sign is that I have clocked and named it – if you name it or give yourself a little compassion as to where it might be coming from, you begin the healing.

You see, as your child grows, they become a reflection of your own experiences of trauma and pain. And in that reflection you begin to see clearly what is and what should not be. It becomes apparent how adults, who should be doing the right thing, protecting and taking on the responsibilities of adulthood, can fail to do so. You start to seriously wonder how and why certain things could've been done to you as your child grows.

My duty, however, as a mother and professional in this area of work, is to do the work on myself and address these issues.

Despite the weight of trauma and the injustices our women have to face, First Nations mothers are determined to redefine parenthood with strength, love and power. We draw upon the resilience of our ancestors, grounding ourselves in the wisdom of our cultural teachings. Healing becomes an act of resistance as we strive to break the cycles of intergenerational trauma and carve out a brighter future for their children. As we continue to grow through this, reclaim our space and exist and survive, we change the cycle by passing down cultural practices and instilling a sense of identity and belonging that strengthens the bond between children and parents, the land and us.

Despite the hardships and injustices, as First Nations mothers we are determined to raise our children with love and fortitude. The wounds of child removal and the agony of hospitals as removal institutions cannot obscure the bond between mothers and our children. Through cultural revitalisation, community support and acts of resistance, First Nations mothers continue to shape a future where their children can grow with strength, love and a profound connection to their heritage with a living, being and doing of sovereignty.

That is who Waitui is – our Bunjdalung Widubul-Wiabul Kaiviti Bati (Indigenous warrior).

The world is hers.

SEPARATING FAMILIES

OVER TIME, IT HAS BECOME evident that the act of separating families through the removal of children is widely misunderstood to be in the best interests of the child. It is important to challenge the notion that these interventions serve the best interests of the child and their families in the long term.

Contrary to popular belief, the outcome of removals is not a guaranteed safe and secure environment for the child involved. It must be said as clearly and directly as possible that when one makes a report or assumes they are creating a better life for the child and family by involving department services and having a child removed, children are not going to magically be placed into a safe home environment.

For children placed into foster care, particularly from First Nations communities in Australia, there exists an alarming pipeline that frequently leads to their involvement in incarceration. This unfortunate trend highlights systemic issues within the foster care system that fails to adequately support and protect these vulnerable children.

Rather than finding a nurturing and supportive environment, many children in foster care are subjected to a cycle of instability, neglect and abuse. We continue to see that children in foster care face a range of challenges including unstable placements, limited access to essential services, emotional trauma and an increased likelihood of encountering the criminal justice system.

The removal of children not only impacts the child but also has profound and lasting effects on their families. Separation can lead to a loss of cultural identity, the severing of relationships and a breakdown of family dynamics. These effects can be especially detrimental to our communities, where the preservation of cultural heritage and connection to community are vital.

Instead of relying solely on removals as a solution, it is crucial to shift the focus towards prevention, supporting families and providing resources that address the root causes of potential harm to children. This approach recognises the importance of wrapping services around families, empowering them to overcome challenges and ensuring that children can remain safely at home whenever possible.

Long yarn short, debunking the myths surrounding removals is essential for a comprehensive understanding of their implications. By acknowledging that the removal of children does not always place them in loving foster homes or lead to a better future or actually work, we can create a better world.

Removing children from Indigenous families is harmful to all individuals and communities. This action is typically viewed as a solution focused solely on the child, but the department and its current procedures often overlook the broader implications and ripple effects on everyone involved. The welfare system has a deeply troubling and painful history within our communities, and as long as it persists in its current form, it will never be accepted or tolerated.

It is imperative to recognise the intersecting crises of housing instability, domestic and family violence, and the broader systemic problems that perpetuate the issues that can lead to child removal. Separating families through the foster care system, while sometimes seen as a quick fix, fails to address the underlying crises caused by systems of oppression.

First Nations families often face significant barriers in accessing safe, affordable and culturally appropriate housing. Discriminatory policies, inadequate funding and limited access to resources contribute to overcrowding, substandard housing conditions and an increased risk of child removal due to perceived neglect. Inadequate housing is often used as a justification for the intervention and removal of Indigenous children from their families.

The bias towards Western standards of living and a lack of cultural competence within child welfare systems perpetuate the cycle of targeting First Nations families, further exacerbating disparities and the high rate of department investigation. The lack of adequate housing contributes to increased surveillance and intervention by child welfare agencies, while policing practices further perpetuate the cycle of systemic oppression and involvement with the child welfare system.

The targeting of First Nation families in out-of-home care through systems of oppression, such as housing and policing, is a deeply rooted issue with far-reaching consequences. It is crucial to recognise and challenge these systems' uneven power dynamics, biases and discriminatory practices.

One deeply concerning aspect of the family policing system is how it often acts as a mechanism to punish poverty. Families facing economic hardship, due to systemic societal inequalities, are disproportionately targeted and separated under the guise of child protection. This practice is not only unjust but also further exacerbates the challenges faced by these vulnerable families.

It is important to recognise that poverty is not a measure of your ability to parent or provide a loving and nurturing environment for your children. Yet, all too often, families who struggle financially are met with judgement, stigma and intervention from child protective services. This punitive approach not only fails to address the root causes of poverty but also perpetuates a cycle of trauma and separation for both parents and children.

Instead of punishing poverty, it is imperative that we reframe our approach and support families in need. Poverty should not be met with punitive measures and removals; rather, it should be met with compassion, understanding and access to comprehensive support systems. These support systems should address the underlying factors that contribute to economic hardship and provide families with resources such as affordable housing, job training, childcare assistance and mental health services.

By shifting our focus to supporting families in need, we can break the cycle of poverty and create an environment in which children can thrive alongside their parents. It is important to recognise that removing children from their families often worsens the challenges faced by impoverished households, rather than resolving them. This approach fails to address the systemic issues that perpetuate poverty, while also traumatising children and parents and potentially leading to long-term negative outcomes for all involved.

Shifting to supporting families in the first instance means providing access to quality education, healthcare, affordable housing and social services. By addressing the root causes of poverty and providing families with the necessary support, we can break the intergenerational cycles of trauma and provide children with the stable and nurturing environments that they deserve. By doing so, we can also strengthen families and ultimately build a society that values the wellbeing and success of all its members.

Domestic and family violence is another critical factor that disproportionately affects marginalised communities. Survivors of domestic violence often face immense challenges when trying to protect themselves and their children. The lack of accessible and affordable housing options, coupled with limited resources and support, can leave survivors trapped in dangerous situations.

In these instances, rather than receiving the necessary assistance and support to heal and rebuild their lives, families may find themselves caught in a cycle of child removal and placement into the foster care system. This cycle fails to address the systemic crises of domestic violence and housing instability, perpetuating further harm and trauma for both parents and children.

It is essential to acknowledge that removing children from their families does not address the root causes of these systemic issues. Instead, it serves as a band-aid solution that fails to address the underlying oppression and structural inequalities that contribute to familial crises.

Addressing these systemic issues requires a multifaceted approach that provides accessible and affordable housing options, comprehensive support services for survivors of domestic violence, and resources that empower families to heal and thrive.

There is also a belief that children wearing dirty clothes means they are being neglected and justifies investigation into their families and the potential removal from their homes. Poverty, lack of access to laundry facilities, mental health issues or overwhelming familial stressors are just some factors that could lead to temporary lapses in caregiving, resulting in children wearing dirty clothes. Quite often, when children have dirty clothes, factors such as socioeconomic status, family status and environment play a role in how one chooses to respond. For example, if a kid from a wealthy family has dirty clothes, they had a fun day; however, if a child from a poor family has dirty clothes, they must be neglected. This stereotype is violent and harmful, and when someone chooses to report as a result, it opens up a door of harm to our people.

A more holistic approach is needed within the foster care system. Instead of relying solely on removals, the system should prioritise working alongside families, providing the necessary support and resources to address the core issues that contribute to child endangerment. This way, families can access the help they need without experiencing the trauma of separation. Ultimately, the goal should be to create a system that supports families in crisis while prioritising the best interests of the child and their long-term welfare.

I have met some beautiful people who choose the pathway of fostering for many well-intentioned reasons. I have relationships with non-Indigenous foster carers who have taken in First Nations children and, ethically, they know this is completely wrong. Often the system states it is their last resort; however, upon critical reflection and accountability, you begin to see actual appropriate efforts were not made.

I have also had some pretty heavy conversations in which non-Indigenous people just did not know their place. Respectfully, I see the way they mean well but, at the same time, I do not see them fighting for, protecting, advocating for and loving the child in their care as if that child was their own. I often see how the system of family policing teaches foster carers to act as substitutes rather than caretakers, meaning that if the situation becomes too rough, it's deemed okay to respond with harm.

When I was in one foster place, there was a little child who I will call Jack. Jack was much younger than I was, and I considered him a little brother. I was always the baby growing up in my community, so I took having another little jarjum to take care of very seriously and did so with all my love.

This young child, Jack, struggled, not because of himself but because of everything around him. He was always spoken about in terms of deficits, diagnoses and punishments. One day, Jack came back to the house and was acting out. It was after a visit to his mum and, just like any child would act, Jack was angry, hurt and upset that he had just been taken away from her again. He went outside and smashed a toy that he knew he could put back together. The foster carers immediately responded with punishment and threatened to call the police. This scared him, and he ran into a corner and didn't want to come out. Jack's history involved police hurting him, scaring him and, like me, taking him from his family.

What those 'carers' didn't know was that Jack had been taught that when he is struggling or having a bad day, it's okay to go outside. Jack also coped with dissociation by breaking things to fix them. He loved fixing things. I remember watching him build so many things, and I would think, *Wow, this kid could be an engineer, builder, anything.* What the system and his foster 'carers' saw as deficits, I saw as strengths that were important to embrace, nurture and work on.

As a mother, if my child had a bad day, there is no way I would threaten to call the police. Have you ever had a bad day? I mean it – have you?

Now, imagine being six years old, scared, terrified, in a stranger's place, having been taken to who knows how many homes before this. Imagine constantly being told you are not good enough, struggling with severe dissociation and having your caretakers respond with threats.

Imagine.

After I ran away at eighteen, I remember speaking to a staff member from Barnardos, which was the non-governmental organisation that held my case. I asked the worker what happened to Jack. I made comments about how awful the carers were. I was later informed that the carers tried to overdose Jack on Ritalin. He was hospitalised and removed from their care.

They were not punished or held criminally liable; they were protected because they used his illness as a weapon against him, and a protection for themselves. They said he was holding scissors, so they took it upon themselves to give him more Ritalin.

After this incident, he was placed in a residential foster home.

I still feel sick to my stomach writing this. I am now twenty-six. I do not know where Jack is, and Jack does not know where I am.

Often, children in the system do not have the privilege to build a consistent connection with each other. It is ripped away from them very quickly.

The incident where the foster carers attempted to overdose Jack with Ritalin is horrific and it represents a severe breach of trust and duty of care. It highlights the potential dangers of placing vulnerable children in the care of people who may not have the necessary knowledge, skills or empathy to support those children's wellbeing. If this occurred in a home environment with biological parents, it would constitute neglect and likely result in removal of the child and potential criminal charges of abuse. The fact that Jack's carers were protected rather than held accountable for their actions illustrates a failure of the system to prioritise the best interests of the child.

The lack of continuity and connection experienced by children like Jack is another significant issue within the foster care system. Relationships are frequently disrupted and severed, preventing children from forming stable and consistent connections. This instability contributes to their feelings of fear, isolation and confusion.

Removing First Nations children from their families and putting them in placements in non-Indigenous or white homes is a stark reminder of the systemic racism embedded within the foster care system. The continued overrepresentation of our communities in foster care highlights the persistent inequities and biases that prevail within the system.

Responsibility and authority should not lie solely in a flawed system like foster care. Placing the burden on a system that has consistently proven ineffective is unfair and detrimental to children and their families. Instead, the focus should be on directing resources towards supporting and empowering families, providing them with the necessary tools, services and assistance to navigate their challenges and keep their families intact.

Completely abolishing the foster care system does not mean abandoning children or disregarding their needs. It means recognising that the current structure is fundamentally flawed and incapable of adequately fulfilling its intended purpose.

Rather than relying on a broken system, it is imperative to invest in alternative approaches that prioritise prevention, support and empowerment for families in need. This involves redirecting funding and resources to programs that focus on family preservation, mental health support, substance abuse treatment and comprehensive social services. It also means not punishing families when they are simply struggling. The extra intersections of race and class often result in punitive measures being the go-to response. As I've mentioned, removal often takes place due to assumptions of neglect; however, if families' needs are met, then the element of neglect would not be present.

I wrote this chapter in the United States, where I had the joy of meeting and working with community. I gave a talk at the University of Pennsylvania on the intersections of human rights and sovereignty from the context of Australia. After the talk, I spoke with attendees, and one staunch person who works with grandmothers in the United States to stop child removal said, 'If something can be fixed with money, don't remove the child.' This simple sentence alone was power.

If something can be fixed with money, don't remove the child.

If we did this, we would see many of our children returned home.

Pay for family support.

Pay for food.

Pay for extra support for children.

Pay for rehabilitation, instead of placing families in the public sector, where waiting is often over a year.

If something can be fixed with money, don't remove the child.

Let me tell you what happens in reality. The money is often provided to foster carers, every means of support and resource, but not where the need can actually be met. Resources, money and support can go a long way for a family. Removal does not go a long way.

Removal and family policing act as the undergraduate degree for a masters in the prison system.

Enough is enough.

TRANSFORMING

THE FAMILY

POLICING SYSTEM

THROUGH MY WORK AS A human rights advocate, lawyer and survivor, I have witnessed the devastating impact on families as they are stripped of their fundamental rights and access to their children. The current system perpetuates the oppression of marginalised communities, particularly First Nations children and young people who are subjected to unjust family policing regimes.

University students often finish their degrees with units championing approaches that do more harm, when the goal should be to not do harm at all. Refusing to participate or actively engage in removal protocols that you know are wrong is a powerful act of individual strength. This also means recognising that when funding is provided through agencies such as the department, there is a real urgency to recognise the strings attached – those strings often being the control of the family policing system.

When we choose to not accept, this means we are choosing not to give them clout and false credibility to reach our communities.

Instead of working for the professional kidnappers and maintaining a system that punishes families, one can choose to participate in the community and work towards creating a better world. One can choose to work in a space that demands the funds committed to removal practices and making the system stronger actually go to making communities stronger.

I am not saying that you shouldn't accept the government funding provided, because the reality is we are placed in a crisis we did not choose to be in. However, we must see a real shift of these funds. Stop funding removals. Stop funding agencies failing to actually meet the needs of Aboriginal and Torres Strait Islander people. We know it does not work. We don't need any more evidence when we see the long-term outcomes of the state's failure to hold parental responsibility. Again, the state is not a parent. The state does not know love.

Back to how important teaching is and its influence: I recall a personal experience during my final law elective. I had enrolled in a children's rights course expecting to learn about the rights of children and young people. However, to my disappointment, the course turned out to be more about the rights of the state and system, promoting the oppression of families and communities.

This particular class took place during the peak of the COVID-19 pandemic and was conducted online. The teacher's perspective was biased and lacked any critical analysis of the racism embedded in the welfare system. Even when discussing the rights of Indigenous children, this white teacher failed to acknowledge that it was not her place to speak on behalf of Indigenous families or understand our experiences and struggles. She further continued to highlight how important removal is.

Throughout this course, I tried to offer my insights as a law student, a survivor and someone actively working with families fighting against the violence of the professional kidnappers. However, as soon as my colleagues – my fellow law students – and I challenged the lecturer's views, we were met with a silenced chat box where no-one could contribute anymore. It became evident that she was not prepared to handle the truth.

It was disheartening to realise that lecturers and professionals within the institution were teaching students to strengthen the system rather than empower communities. This realisation was truly heartbreaking. But it also highlighted the importance of refusing to participate in actions that perpetuate harm and seeking ways to strengthen communities instead. If and when appropriate, we should share our knowledge and support the community. We must never forget that doing harm will lead to exclusion and a lack of welcome.

I reflect on this, and I reflect on the solidarity and strength we had as a class, as other law students and I questioned her.

There was power in doing this together. To this day, I am proud to have taken that class with staunch people who care, and that's the win. People care, and people can show up in numbers.

Refusing to participate in actions that continue harm, such as working for child removal bodies, and choosing to do things in a better way that strengthens communities is not only commendable but also necessary. The harm caused by these systems and departments cannot be overlooked.

When we make the department stronger, we inadvertently risk the safety and wellbeing of our children. These institutions often prioritise bureaucratic procedures and policies over the actual needs and experiences of families and communities.

Through my work, I have also learned that people in positions of bureaucratic power are often told a different story to what is actually taking place on the ground. The focus becomes more on punishment rather than support, coercion rather than empowerment.

There is a lack of lens, and a genuine fear to drive actual change. The fear being: 'Well, what if a child dies?'

Let me tell you this.

We are at the worst-case scenario.

When we look at Black deaths in custody, when we hear the stories of youth prisons and how the majority of these children sitting with care and protection orders, we have failed.

We are at the worst-case scenario.

By refusing to be a part of these harmful systems and instead working towards community-based solutions, we can make a significant impact. Strengthening communities involves recognising and addressing the root causes of issues, providing resources and support to families, and promoting collaboration and unity. It is through these actions that we can create a safer and more nurturing environment for our children.

The root, in this instance, is the department, and I mean it. It truly starts with tackling family policing departments, because if you strengthen a family to be supported with their children, you will change outcomes. There is a big focus on 'crime', but if we shift this to supporting families, generations and communities, we change everything.

Going back to my childhood years, specifically my final years at Malabar Primary School, I must share that there was one exceptional case worker I remember: Anne. She genuinely wanted the best for my family, and looking back I can see how torn she was between the harmful system and recognising the love within my family.

Anne would pick me up from the foster placement I was in at the early hour of 5:30 am to get me to Malabar. She really did not want me to be uprooted and taken to another school – another change and another struggle for my heart.

I grew a love for her very old car, which she named Beau. During our drives, we listened to music, shared stories and even became friends with a local who had a horse along the way. Every morning, I would eagerly anticipate seeing the horse. It became an integral part of my unstable childhood, offering a sense of comfort and stability. I would bring an apple each day and give the horse a gentle pat.

Anne truly went above and beyond her duties, or maybe she just did her duty the right way. I had many awful social workers who failed me. That's what I feel anyway. I believe that Anne's heart was always in the right place, but like any job, when the spirit knows it is engaged in something wrong, it becomes exhausted much quicker. A heart can't feel too good if it's stealing and participating in a system that breaks families and communities.

In our way, we know a lot of these people will get spiritually sick. When you are doing harm to our people, our old people are watching everything. But sickness will come. Hurt one of us, hurt all of us. The spirit knows.

In reflecting on Anne's actions, I see the genuine care she had for my family. However, it is unfortunate that she was limited by the constraints of the system she worked within. Despite her efforts, the harmful practices of the child welfare system ultimately overshadowed her intentions. This experience serves as a reminder that even the most well-meaning individuals can become weary when they are a part of a system that perpetuates harm.

I don't know the complete reason, but I again had another change in social workers. In my adult years, I bumped into

Anne, and she said how proud she is of me, and when I told her Mum and Dad died, she was gutted. I still don't know why things had to change, but they did. And sadly, my job as a kid in the foster system was to just go with it.

It is my belief that our goal should not be to strengthen the power of the state, but rather to step aside and empower our communities to thrive. Let me be clear: I'm not suggesting that we simply dump all responsibilities onto the community, especially considering the immense historical trauma and harm inflicted upon our people. However, we must acknowledge our responsibility in creating a world that upholds self-determination and allows for community-controlled progress, goals and processes.

One way to address this is by defunding the family policing system and redirecting those funds towards the community. Additionally, we need to restructure oversight mechanisms to ensure that when it comes to First Nations children subject to family policing, the early stages of intervention involve community members working with one another, not solely relying on the state.

Decolonisation demands serious attention. The settler-colonial state, through its historical violence and contemporary forms of child removal, perpetuates the violence we witness today. The carceral state is merely an extension of the historical settler state, where bias, prediction and surveillance serve as tools for state intervention, leading to the destruction of families for generations to come.

Surveillance in the context of child removal must be viewed through the lens of case workers assuming the role of police officers. This is why I refer to it as family policing, as it starts with the surveillance of families. The problem lies in the fact that case workers often take it upon themselves to decide what is right or wrong and ultimately to mete out punishment or support.

Their judgements are often based on biased reporting and are frequently linked to racism. They rely on their own perceptions and predictions of what might happen, without considering the unique circumstances and needs of the families they are supposed to support. This kind of surveillance maintains a system of control and creates a cycle in which families are unfairly targeted and punished based on subjective judgements. It is essential that we address this and identify the role of those working, in practice, as tools of punishment.

Imagine you are a single father living in a housing commission in New South Wales, and a case worker from the department knocks on your door.

You answer, and the case worker tells you she needs to come in. She got a call and report from your daughter's school. It really is not that serious, but she will have to ask you and your daughter some questions. She also needs to talk to your other child, and she will need to take a look around the house, just to make sure you have everything you need. That's fine with you, right? Reluctantly, with fear, you let her in. You don't verbally say yes, but you nod your head. You are actually speechless that the department has rocked up to your place.

You watch her take notes as she opens the kitchen cabinets and refrigerator door, counting the food products available, looking at the bread to see if it's gone out of date. You see her come across the number of beer bottles left in the refrigerator.

You hesitate – should you explain to her why they are there, should you let her know people have been over? But then you fear this means overcrowding and neglect in her eyes. Should you let her know this? She has moved on, though, smelling smoke. You ask yourself, should you let her know that windows are open and the neighbours smoke next door and it sometimes comes in?

The case worker begins to dramatically step over the toys that the kids, and your nieces and nephews have thrown around the living room. She scribbles in her pad, taking notes as she walks by the sink, which is full of dirty dishes that you have not had time to clean – and, yes, there's not much dish soap left because it is expensive and your payday is in a few days.

She walks into your bedroom, then your kids' room in the housing commission flat, and then the bathroom, taking notes the whole time. The house is messy. You struggle with this. The case worker calls your daughter into the bedroom and asks you to instruct her that it's okay to speak alone and that she should follow the case worker's instructions and answer any questions she might have. Nine-year-olds may not feel comfortable speaking with strangers, of course. You follow these instructions, worried. You don't even know your rights, but you are fearful by this point and walk back to the kitchen table. Your daughter then looks at you to see whether this is okay. She listens to her dad, always.

What choice do you have, really?

The case worker finishes with your daughter and now calls in your eleven-year-old son. You want to ask what is going on, if you are free to go or better still if she would just leave your family alone, but you are scared that what happened to your other family members – like the stories of your own nan – will happen to you too. When she is finished speaking to you and your kids, the case worker leaves and tells you that you will hear from her soon.

It's now upon her to determine whether your children are taken or not.

This is what happens when the department begins to surveil your home, and this is still happening to low-income First Nations families in Australia today.

In this story, I am the daughter, and the father is my dad.

From the very beginning of this book, I've shared how the department intruded on my family without invitation from the moment I was born. And this intrusion persisted for years. In fact, ten-and-a-half years.

It involved unexpected visits and calculated surveillance, which ultimately led to my removal. Every observation and note taken was weaponised against my family, in court and beyond. The case workers assumed the role of professional storytellers, narrating tales that often went unchallenged and were accepted as truth in the legal process.

Even when I had very rare visits to see my family, it was under surveillance. I remember when a stranger arrived at my mum's Elphinstone Road housing commission flat. This stranger observed my family and every room, making notes on whether I 'looked' safe in my own mother's home. I came across the 'assessment' when I was twenty-five years old. The notes were awful and discriminatory towards my parents and continued to argue that my best interests would be served by me remaining a ward of the state.

Case workers are entrusted with the responsibility of upholding the state's child welfare laws. However, it is concerning that many of these individuals lack significant experience and are making crucial final decisions regarding whether to dismantle families, punish them due to their poverty or provide support. These actions are mandated in New South Wales by the *Children and Young Persons (Care and Protection) Act 1998* and through other legislation throughout the different states and territories in Australia.

As tools of the state, these case workers are tasked with investigating every report of child maltreatment, regardless of its source, through the state's ROSH reporting processes, despite the racism that often leads to these reports, or the racism in the bias, prediction and action to take 'emergency' removals. These investigations often involve searching the family's home, just like the search I just described. These individuals, who are essentially strangers, enter homes without clear, prior informed consent and hold the authority to disrupt the fundamental rights of family integrity.

They possess statutory power to either remove children based on their own authority or facilitate emergency removals or the implementation of court orders, resulting in children being taken away from their families and placed into foster care, residential facilities, hotels with strangers or, in horrific cases, prison. This can ultimately lead to the permanent severing of family relationships through the termination of parental rights, drastically altering the futures of children.

I spent from the age of ten-and-a-half to eighteen having my childhood stolen from me – a significant period of time in a child's life.

As I reflect on this time, it brings me immense pain. I am reminded of how the system deprived my family and community of crucial moments, those times when memories are made and stories are shared between parents, children and their community. All of that was taken away from me.

In 2023, our communities united to protest against the forced closure of the National Centre of Indigenous Excellence, a significant place for many of our children that was already experiencing the effects of gentrification and isolation. Our advocacy efforts were consistent, with the entire community actively participating. However, amid this collective action, I had a distressing encounter.

An Aboriginal case worker named Gloria, who had taken me away years ago, recognised me. She played a big role in stealing me and harming my community. She approached me and my daughter and remarked, 'That baby looks like Alby ... Vanessa, you also resemble your father.'

I immediately identified her and felt a wave of sickness. When she attempted to embrace my baby, I firmly said, 'Do not touch my child. I am not prepared to face you or be in this moment with you.' Unaware of the trauma and heartache she had caused, she seemed puzzled by my response. I continued, 'You took me away from my father, and he's no longer here. You are not the hero in this story or a good person.'

My partner, Ellia, sensing my distress, suggested we leave, and reassured me, 'You are safe, bub.'

I disclosed to him, 'That woman took me.' The last memory I'd had of her was when she knocked on our door all those years ago and stole me.

It is concerning that Gloria thought she had the access and right to be in contact with me, to have a conversation, that she even felt in any way we were on any kind of terms, and – the most triggering and harmful thing – that she attempted to interact with my child.

This incident highlights that many case workers are unaware of the lasting harm caused by their actions. She probably thought she did the right thing, and that's the problem. One reactive decision, instead of proactive, or one racist decision, to remove an Aboriginal child from their family, community and place, has worse long-term consequences.

When I reflect on this as an adult, I wonder how she sleeps at night, knowing that she ripped an Aboriginal child from her family.

How does one sleep knowing your job is to break families apart? Knowing that you are contributing to greater harm than love? Knowing that while a fast decision has been made, that there are serious long-term consequences to be had?

How does one sleep knowing that you have created more barriers for families? That you are about to drag a family, most likely a *struggling* family, through courts and systems, and subject them to more racism?

It would have been cheaper to say, 'How can I help? Do you need or want my help?'

It would have been better to say, 'Hey, we aren't here to take Vanessa. We are here offering a hand, proper resources.'

It would have been better to not add to the disempowerment, but to instead empower.

Work with, not against.

Imagine we offered a little more of our love and ethics instead of punishment.

Imagine.

As a survivor of this system, I have learned many things, but most importantly I have come to understand that the path to ending the disproportionate rates of child removal and incarceration, and the ongoing form of modern enslavement in Australia via the family policing system lies in abolition.

I pursued studies in law and social work to gain a better understanding of this system. Even as a child, I was always driven to understand why people do the things they do. It was important for me to comprehend the law and the ways in which these systems continue to target First Nations and marginalised families.

With my professional background, personal experiences and knowledge of the system, I keep arriving at the same conclusion. We can absolutely work towards non-reformist reforms. This means, as we approach the horizon for change, we can aim for wins that do not necessarily make the state stronger.

Non-reformist reforms in the family policing and child welfare space are innovative approaches that seek to address systemic issues and create lasting change, rather than just adjusting existing structures. These reforms challenge the status quo and aim to transform the way child welfare systems operate.

Instead of making minor adjustments or applying band-aid solutions, non-reformist reform advocates for radical changes that address the root causes of problems within the child welfare system.

Examples of non-reformist reform in this space include restructuring funding models to prioritise prevention and community-based services over removal and placement, implementing culturally responsive practices that centre the voices and experiences of marginalised communities, and reimagining the role of case workers to focus on supporting families rather than policing them.

By embracing non-reformist reforms, the family policing system can move towards creating more equitable and just outcomes for children and families, working towards a future where all individuals have access to the support and resources they need to thrive.

It must be acknowledged that instead of seeking to merely improve or reform existing systems, non-reformist reforms aim to dismantle oppressive structures and create alternative approaches that address the root causes of injustice. It is a key feature of the abolitionist movement, and it is not impossible.

Traditional reforms often focus on making minor adjustments to existing systems while maintaining the fundamental power dynamics and structures that perpetuate harm. Non-reformist reforms, on the other hand, challenge the status quo by questioning the very foundations upon which these systems are built.

Family policing and incarceration are institutional systems deeply rooted in racism, capitalism and social control, and their very existence enacts harm and violence.

Non-reformist reforms challenge us to think beyond superficial changes and to strive for transformational shifts that address the underlying causes of these problems. Non-reformist reforms encourage us to question the necessity and effectiveness of punitive measures, encouraging alternatives that prioritise restorative justice, healing and community support. They prompt us to imagine and create systems that prevent harm and provide resources and support to marginalised communities.

The horizon of non-reformist reforms is a future where systems of punishment and oppression are replaced with holistic, community-centred approaches that address the root causes of harm. It is a vision that requires us to fundamentally reshape our understanding of justice, focusing on accountability, restoration and transformative change.

This horizon invites us to envision a society in which all individuals can thrive without the need for oppressive institutions.

The horizon is love. Love for each other, for our families and communities.

It's our greatest act of genuine care for each other.

There is a brighter world waiting to be imagined and, when we actively work towards building that new world, we will bring our children back home where they truly belong.

I hope it is no longer just an imagining, but a doing – now. And I see that with the love of community.

In our pursuit of social justice, we often encounter moments that test our emotional, political and personal boundaries. However, when we thrive together with our communities and loved ones, engaging in conversations that hold us accountable, even when we may be wrong, we learn the true meaning of reconciliation and embracing abolition as a practice.

Feedback becomes critical in reshaping our work and moving forward with purpose. I acknowledge when I am wrong, and my heart is open to the people I love to provide feedback, and with caution to those I don't love but do have time for feedback. I try not to respond with denial, but openness to learn and hopefully get it right.

I have gone from being a kid in a care system that doesn't actually care at all to being appointed as the inaugural commissioner for Aboriginal and Torres Strait Islander Children and Young people.

The role exists because the people before me fought for it. Ultimately, it's an example of non-reformist reform. It is the first of its kind and came about through both formal and community processes.

I now hold independent statutory oversight, but while I maintain this role, it will be led by the community – especially those I represent: First Nations children and young people.

When discussing abolition, many people express fear and hesitancy towards this concept. They may deem it as too extreme or radical, believing it to be unattainable. However, I want to emphasise that advocating for the wellbeing of our jarjums, families and communities is not radical. I was first introduced to this idea through conversations with Aunty Anne Cregan, who provided me with a home in a time of need. I crossed paths with Aunty Anne while attending an event at the Gilbert + Tobin law firm following a protest addressing the mistreatment of Indigenous children in Don Dale Youth Detention Centre in the Northern Territory. I was accompanying my friend who was participating in a moot (a mock judicial proceeding).

I encountered Aunty Anne Cregan engrossed in editing documents related to the Royal Commission into the Protection and Detention of Children in the Northern Territory. Instantly, I was enveloped by her warmth and compassion. She truly embodies love. Who would have thought that a year or so later I would be working in her team.

Aunty Anne knew my pain, and if I am being honest she is one of the most exceptional legal, personal and spiritual human beings I have ever met, and I am so lucky to know her. Aunty Anne and I would stay up for hours talking about the new world. We would envision new ways of practice and doing. She bought me an abolition book to draft all my ideas in. She often encourages me to write them down and plan them out.

Often when we hear the word *abolition*, we apply it to the prison system discourse, but in my work and what I have researched and learned is that this so deeply applies to the statutory child 'protection' system. I talk more about this in my TEDx talk, 'A state is not a parent: Why the child welfare system fails'.

In Australia, the statutory child removal system has deep-rooted connections with the carceral state, perpetuating a pipeline to prison for First Nations children in out-of-home care. By shedding light on the interplay between child removal, incarceration and the violence within these systems, we can begin to understand the urgent need for transformative change.

The statutory child removal system, primarily operated by child protection agencies, exercises extensive powers to investigate allegations of child maltreatment and remove children from their families. Unfortunately, this system disproportionately targets First Nations families, reflecting deeply entrenched racial biases. The overrepresentation of First Nations children in out-of-home care is a damning consequence of this. Once removed, these children are thrust into a system that powers a cycle of violence and marginalisation.

The carceral state, encompassing the criminal and juvenile justice systems, thrives on punitive approaches, authoritarian control and confinement. It enacts violence through the over-policing and over-incarceration of marginalised communities, including First Nations peoples. The disproportionate representation of First Nations children within the youth justice system is a clear indication of how these intersecting systems perpetuate the pipeline to prison.

The pipeline to prison operates through various mechanisms. Firstly, the trauma and disruption caused by child removal leave lasting impacts on children's wellbeing, mental health and social development. This trauma often manifests in behavioural issues and contributes to subsequent targeting in the criminal justice system by the state. Moreover, children in out-of-home care face a lack of stable support networks, limited access to education and inadequate aftercare, all of which increase their vulnerability, criminalisation and experiences of the racism entrenched in society that subjects children and young people to severe risk of over-policing.

It is crucial to recognise that the pipeline to prison for First Nations children in out-of-home care is a result of entrenched systemic racism and neglect. To create change, it is imperative to shift the focus from punitive measures to comprehensive and culturally sensitive support systems. This includes investing in community-led initiatives, strengthening cultural connections and involving First Nations communities in decision-making processes surrounding child welfare.

The connection between the statutory child removal system and the carceral state reveals a dark reality for First Nations children in out-of-home care. This pipeline to prison perpetuates violence, reinforcing systemic inequalities and robbing these children of their futures. Urgent systemic abolition of department bodies is needed to address the root causes and create a more just and equitable society centred on healing, support and empowerment for First Nations families.

Through collective action and by dismantling these interconnected systems, we can pave the way for a brighter future for all children.

As a survivor, I implore you not to remain silent. This is the essence of abolition. It entails choosing to act with tenderness, love and justice. It involves taking a stand against sexual violence and abuse, seeking restorative practices for all, and envisioning new ways to operate in a society that often views its members as disposable. Abolition means supporting our youth, particularly young women of colour, especially in the face of a government that targets children and young people. Abolition is putting education into practice and recognising that a better world is possible.

Authentic abolition serves and protects our loved ones. It fights for access to adequate and quality healthcare for all families. The current healthcare systems are responsible for too many deaths among my people, as racial violence is deeply ingrained in the fabric of Australian society. Abolition means not relying on the police as first responders to mental and emotional health crises. It advocates against imprisonment and excessive policing.

Abolition does not dictate how people should live their lives. It does not claim moral superiority over our people and those we care for. Rather, it emphasises community, inclusivity and finding ways to repair the damage caused by necessary separations. It acknowledges enabling behaviours and offers tools to prevent them. Abolition does not take sides but rather stands alongside the community. When we embrace this approach, we also embrace the essential task of teaching our children how to hold space for their emotions instead of suppressing them out of fear of punishment. We must also recognise the state itself being a perpetrator.

I recall being punished and experiencing abuse while in care as a child. This had such a profound impact that I questioned my ability to become a parent. Abolition entails teaching our children about accountability and reminding them of their inherent freedom. I won't ever take freedom away from my daughter.

Here in Australia, we proudly incarcerate children as well as punish their families and communities when a perceived 'risk' is identified. We do this by separating the child from their parents and community, falsely claiming that the state will then serve as their parent.

If we implement a new practice centred in care and dignity we might find a way to challenge our instinct to 'cancel' each other and punish the most vulnerable. Abolition is about how we treat one another and how we show up in relationships. It involves responding to harm caused and harm received, distinguishing between the large-scale systems and individuals that inflict harm.

Abolition is not about bullying; it's about standing up for oneself with love. We must build a culture rooted in care, dignity and accountability. In fact, this culture is already built in our communities so beautifully and with warmth.

We need people like you, people who are willing to educate themselves and demand justice for the children who are taken away from their families. We need your help to dismantle the family policing system that forcibly places children for adoption without parental consent, removes children at birth and continues to surveil families.

Use your platform to write, speak out and support efforts when a First Nations child is taken from country after seeking safety on her traditional lands with her mother. Demand their safety and return home.

Make room for community and understand that, as a visitor, you have the power to stand collectively for change. We need to build our numbers, apply pressure and challenge the treatment of our people as a fundamental issue, recognising that our systems of wellbeing and existence extend far beyond the colonial legal system as a sufficient response to any crises or need.

Black Lives Matter. Black children matter. Black mothers matter. Black fathers matter. Black healing matters. Black love matters. Black air matters. Black breath matters. When officers take the lives and breath away from Black bodies and our people die in custody, *you* must recognise that *we* matter.

But if you choose to show up, I ask that you do it with love. We stand strong and never give up. We demand justice, knowing that this is true love.

The family policing system in Australia and globally is an extension of the carceral system and fails to address other social issues that impact children and families. The state's intervention in our communities only reinforces white supremacy and racism, dictating what constitutes a 'proper' family.

My people have been caretakers since the first sunrise, looking after the land, our people and our children. Our way has always been rooted in deep love and in our cultural practices of being and doing. We continue to raise our children with these sovereign protocols, recognising that our people were the first to highlight developmental stages.

Our survival is not due to the colony but to our role as teachers, caregivers and community builders. Our ability to resist, remain and love.

Since the Stolen Generations, the rates of First Nations children being removed have risen significantly. The origins of child removal and state intervention in our lives can be traced back to the invasion. The forced separation of families and control of Black children through removal have been instruments used to destroy our fundamental connections as First Nations people.

Our way of life, rooted in healing, harmony and survival, threatened the invaders. Even today, we are still targeted by the same system. The system is not broken; it is perfectly designed.

Racism often plays a significant role in how child welfare departments, like the Department of Communities and Justice, operate. Mandatory reporters, such as teachers and doctors, make decisions regarding reports of suspected child maltreatment, often influenced by racism. These welfare bodies do nothing to address the high rates of child and family poverty, the need for affordable housing or the underlying structural inequities that harm children and families.

As an adult survivor, I feel the pain of my experiences as a child, and I reflect on the moments and joy that were taken away from me. As Blackfullas, we continue to have so much taken from us. While those around us are killed by the state, the pain we experience as survivors persists. As adults, we create and hold on to memories that we pass down and share with our families. But the trauma and pain that remain within us should not consume our adult years, taking away our time and energy.

When I was forcibly removed from my father and community, I was stolen from moments. Moments of seeking advice from my mum, connecting with my dad and siblings, and experiencing the joy of being with my family. I was stolen from the everyday routines and experiences that shape us as individuals and families.

The system has never worked and will not work for us. It is designed to break us. Society should not respond with punitive measures but with effective support.

As an adult, when I reflect, I feel pain. Sometimes, this pain takes me back to the moments when my inner child experienced traumatic events. Often, the body holds on to the trauma and pain that linger inside. My therapist explains that the brain is like a filing cabinet, smart enough to retain everything until it can no longer do so, or until we are ready for those things to resurface. Our minds do all they can to protect us.

I deeply reflect on my experiences as a child and remember all the moments of joy that were taken away from me. As Blackfullas, we continue to have so much taken from us. While lives around us continue to be lost at the hands of the state, those who remain also carry enduring pain.

I often question when we will have our utopia back. As adults, especially when we have children of our own, we thrive on memories. Memories that we create to pass down or share with our families.

I recall the memories from before the state forcibly removed me. When I reflect on my experiences from ages ten-and-a-half to eighteen, it feels like a blur, as if the world fast-forwarded to the present. I know this is my mind's way of protecting me from those difficult years as a ward of the state, but it is also a reminder of the pain that no child or person should have to spend their adult years processing, as it robs us of time.

Over the years the department has changed its name, almost as though it is some instant fix for better outcomes. It isn't.

In New South Wales alone, the name has gone from the Aborigines Protection Board (also known as The Board) to Welfare to the Department of Child Safety to the Department of Family and Community Services to the Department of Communities and Justice.

Merely mentioning the department's names to our people can evoke pain in our elders' and parents' eyes and instil fear in children, given the ways these institutional and departmental family policing bodies have harmed us.

Changing the name is often used to imply a change in conduct or a new 'framework'. However, in practice, this is never the case.

The raw reality is that the system must be completely abolished. It has never worked for us, and it never will. The family policing system is designed to break us.

As humans, we have been conditioned to believe that we must follow structures and listen to those in positions of power. But let me make this long yarn short: it is those in positions of power, such as the state and its tools, who have abused those positions and continue to mistreat the people on the receiving end.

As a society, responding to issues with punitive measures instead of effective support simply does not make sense.

Far too many children are being shuffled from one foster placement or residential facility or hotel to another and subjected to even more harmful circumstances. That means you are likely to be moving from one home to another as the department fights to keep you in their care, while your parents fight in court to bring you back home.

Can you imagine if we put those funds towards parental and housing support? Every day, my parents showed up in court to fight for me. My mother, battling her illness, faced the added challenge of fighting for her daughter. Throughout the court proceedings, my mother remained stable. However, everything seemed to be against my parents.

I write this book as a survivor who understands the practice both as a victim of child removal and as someone who has studied law and social work. I have come to realise that Australia is woefully behind in recognising and respecting the rights and voices of Indigenous people. The family policing system is growing and deeply troubling.

When I was forcibly taken, I distinctly remember feeling that my voice was never at the centre, never heard or responded to. The professionals who were supposed to do their jobs prioritised punishment over support. They punished my family, my community and myself.

As a community, when faced with deep pain and injustice, you will find us gathering. We come together to step into our power because that is who we are and who we have always been.

The reason I dedicate myself to this work and give my full heart to the fight is because I get it. I understand it, and I've lived it.

I distinctly remember the moment I was torn from my father's arms that night, and the deep pain and heartache in my father's tears.

As a child, you survive.

As an adult, you never forget.

As my therapist says, my body will always remember, but one thing I know for sure is that I have emerged even stronger – thanks to my ancestors, not the state. Because I am here to free others.

Empowerment – not penalty – should underpin the approach to addressing families and communities within the family policing system. By emphasising strengths, supporting cultural identity, fostering community engagement and providing accessible resources and services, we can create a system that is proactive, inclusive and focused on family preservation.

Empowerment must be led by community and not by the system built to do what we are witnessing today. It is best achieved through community-led initiatives that actively involve families and communities in decision-making processes. By engaging community members in program design, implementation and evaluation, we ensure that services and support are culturally relevant, accessible and responsive to community needs.

Time and time again, I see the love of community give solutions. They must be listened to. When you have a people that make up over 40 per cent of a system, but just 3.5 per cent of the nation, there is a responsibility to involve those people in the decision-making.

In the current child welfare system, resources are often disproportionately allocated towards child removal and out-of-home care. Redirecting those funds to support community needs aims to address the urgent number of child neglect cases by shifting the system's resources – and therefore its focus.

When it comes to department intervention, neglect is often given as the foundational reason for removal. This often keeps it ambiguous as to what the neglect actually is. Recognising that neglect is often the result of systemic issues – such as poverty, lack of affordable housing and limited access to healthcare – means that policies and interventions should prioritise providing families with the support they need to overcome these challenges.

This could involve offering financial assistance, housing support, quality healthcare, and mental health services and support. By investing in community liberation and emphasising prevention, we can work towards creating a more equitable and proactive approach.

If there is allocated funding for removal, it will be used for that. This results in the overemphasis on removals we tend to see. The same goes for incarceration. If there are new prisons built, the beds will be filled.

The focus on child removal and putting children and young people into out-of-home care places significant strain on families and perpetuates a cycle of trauma. The current system often fails to address the root causes of neglect, resulting in high caseloads for social workers and limited resources for preventative measures. If we allocate those funds directly to the needs of the community, shifting our focus away from removal and punitive responses, we will begin to see changes.

Redirecting funds towards prevention and early intervention initiatives allows for a proactive approach in addressing child neglect. If governments invest in community-based programs that provide education, parenting support, mental health services and access to basic necessities, families can receive the necessary tools to prevent 'neglectful' situations as identified by the state. In other words, anything that can be provided to support the family and not result in a removal, so their definition of neglect cannot be used against the family.

Shifting resources from child removal and out-of-home care to community liberation presents an opportunity to meet urgent community needs. It is an investment in the wellbeing, stability and liberation of families, leading to better outcomes for children and our communities.

The court system plays a crucial role in the out-of-home care sector, serving as the ultimate arbiter in determining the fate of children and families involved in child welfare proceedings. Judges and courts must be educated and culturally aware, understanding the impacts and biases at play between the state and the family. By promoting fairness, equity and cultural sensitivity in decision-making, the court system can contribute to positive outcomes for families and promote the preservation of cultural connections. I am seeing a change in how the rights of children and young people are met in the courtroom, but we do have a long way to go.

The primary goal of the court system should be the preservation of families whenever possible, ensuring that the removal of children from their homes is a last resort. Judges should be committed to understanding the dynamics of family systems, recognise the impact of separation on children and actively seek alternatives to out-of-home care.

I further encourage a greater recognition of survivors of family policing whose own children are at risk of state intervention, and for the onus to be placed back on to the department. The fact that the department is often taking the children of parents who were also subject to removal is a clear indicator, again, of their failure to parent and raise children in the state system.

The state simply cannot be a parent. The state knows no love. It will never nourish the beings of the little people, especially when its roots begin in the history of a nation built on stealing kids. It is raising children in its system who will likely become subject to prison or mental health facilities, and who continue to know *no* care or love from that system.

The department often takes away a removed child's own rights to reproduction and child rearing, and we commonly see birth removals between the ages of zero to two years of age occur for new parents who themselves have been the subject of forcible removal. This is because the department automatically deems them inadequate, unstable and unable to raise a child.

In my own experience, having my family or extended kin involved could have made a difference. I suggest that the courts work out means of involving elders and community, so that if a First Nations child is the focus, the community holds greater weight and has direct communication and transparency with judges and those in decision-making positions. I must say though, my kin, my Aunty Colleen, my cousin Pete, my pop, they all tried to get me home. They all tried. My elders wanted me home, and my family wanted me home. However, through constant exclusion processes, their involvement was denied and therefore the fight was between the state and my parents – and we know the state is far more powerful, and often violent.

In talking about kinship, we must be careful of the way our language is becoming weaponised by the department. For example, what I tend to see is the department make statements about children being with their *kin*, but in reality they are with their non-Indigenous siblings and family, and still denied the very objective of kinship: access to culture, community and wellbeing. Kinship must not be weaponised. Kinship systems stem from Indigenous principles of practice, doing and being.

I see the way this is often abused in the process. Kin is our way, is our healing. Kin is our future, kin is our past, kin is our belonging.

Children have a fundamental right to be connected to their communities and traditional lands. For First Nations children, this connection goes beyond personal belonging; it encompasses cultural, spiritual and ancestral ties that are critical to their identity, their wellbeing and the preservation of their rights as First Nations people. The impact of child removal on Indigenous sovereignty, rights and interests is crucial to our future.

Our culture is deeply rooted in our lands and communities. Maintaining a connection to these spaces is vital for our children to learn their language, traditions, ceremonies and practices, ensuring cultural continuity and the passing down of ancestral knowledge. While Australia continues to have a dark history of silencing my people, our children continue to be the future, reclaiming language and belonging.

Children thrive when they have a strong sense of identity and belonging. Being raised within their communities and on their lands allows children to develop a solid foundation rooted in their cultural heritage, history and community values. Our babies have a place, and removal damages all of this.

First Nations communities have an inherent right to self-governance and self-determination. Child removal and the family policing system disrupts these rights and erodes the sovereignty of First Nations people, as it removes future generations from their rightful place within their communities and the role they play in giving back and protecting the mother spirit (the land).

Our kids belong with community.

A CALL TO ARMS

DO NOT MAKE THE STATE stronger.

When I began to write this book, my daughter, Waitui, was only eight months old – a living reminder of the collective grief and anguish we experience as First Nations individuals in the face of racism. I am often reflecting on my daughter's world, her future and what it looks like for all our children.

The system we currently have denies First Nations children the fair and just process they deserve, burdening them with the label of guilty until proven innocent – and often even after that. Our lives are constantly under threat; we are hunted on every scale imaginable.

I intentionally adopt the term *hunted* because it accurately describes the pattern of violence that relentlessly pursues our people. The report on the Royal Commission into Aboriginal Deaths in Custody that came out in 1991 sheds light on the alarming details of how First Nations lives were cut short – not by accident or natural causes, but by our being chased, hunted and murdered by the very authorities tasked with protecting us.

As a mother, lawyer, advocate and survivor, I have come to realise that the reality for our children, our people, is one of constant danger. I firmly believe in the power of protest, not only for fostering human connection and building solidarity but also for challenging the moral compass and power structures that uphold injustice. We can care for many things all at once. That is solidarity.

People turn to protests and social movements as a means of reclaiming power and influencing change when traditional avenues fail them. Often the mass numbers in protest, even if the numbers are small, lead to change. Protests exist as a means to disrupt institutional powers, and they particularly have a place for those who cannot access the institutional powers. Protests remind those in positions of power that our voices matter, that our sheer numbers cannot be ignored.

My new role as the ACT's Aboriginal and Torres Strait Islander Children and Young People Commissioner, which started in February 2024, exists solely because of the people. It is the people who demanded change, who fought tirelessly for the fundamental rights that continue to be denied.

Every day, our voices are silenced, disregarded as inconsequential. But they do matter, and it is through collective struggles against violence and suffering that we find strength and unity. We also discover unity through shared joy and through our unwavering demand for a better world.

In my field of work, I staunchly advocate for abolitionist-oriented reforms, and I believe change is achievable. This includes reallocating funds from family policing – or what many know as *child protection* – budgets towards community development initiatives, while simultaneously working out ways to free our children and young people from prisons and residential facilities that fail to adequately meet their needs. These facilities often cram multiple children together under the supervision of unskilled workers who cannot effectively address the urgent needs of these vulnerable individuals.

These systems, such as incarceration of children and young people, are not the long- or short-term solutions for a better world – a world where we respond to children and young people with care. Decarceration does not mean that we do not care about the problems that may occur or that we are playing down the seriousness of offences. Rather, it requires us to get creative in our thinking, in our ways of doing and responding. Because what we do know for certain is that the current regime does *not* work. So, together, we must be prepared to make these changes, now.

Moreover, urgent reforms must be made that contribute towards abolition, including the elimination of police from the process of child removal. This approach mirrors my own painful story, where I was made to feel like a criminal the night

I was forcefully taken away. I also argue against the involvement of welfare workers acting like police officers, invading homes without warrants or consent, conducting biased and racially motivated 'welfare checks' and deeming families unfit based on false notions of instability or 'neglect'.

This form of policing and surveillance is inherently violent and has no place in our future.

I yearn for a world where our people can freely roam our ancestral lands, unhindered by oppression. But the harsh reality is that we are not free, and this breaks my heart. Rather than providing support, this country prefers to cage individuals, subject them to murder and punish them for their poverty.

It is my deepest hope and fight that we can collectively work towards a future that embraces justice and equity, and truly respects the rights and lives of all people.

I address this crisis and the interconnectedness of various factors for many reasons, but primarily to highlight the damaging impact of the family policing system and the removal of First Nations children. These actions create deep-rooted pain that often leads to the incarceration or targeting of my people. The removal of our people lies at the core of the ongoing violence we face.

Unfortunately, we have not done enough to adequately support families, nor have we fully grasped the risks and harms associated with child removal. When you take a child, you are taking sovereignty, their role, their connection – you are taking whole communities that live inside that little being.

True understanding, taking the time to genuinely comprehend why someone does something, allows for empathy to replace anger. It unveils heartbreaking stories that are often kept silent.

The suppression of our people's voices is yet another way in which we are silenced. If you knew the reasons behind these actions, if you understood the stories and the truth, deep down you too would recognise the profound wrongness of it all.

The brutal truth is that we are not safe – and neither are our children and kin.

'Say their name.'

'Black Lives Matter.'

'Black children matter.'

'Black healing matters.'

These rallying cries for justice and resilience are more than mere words. When we say 'Say their name', it signifies a connection to the deep stories and the importance of remembering the lives taken by state violence. While the perpetrators, often the state itself, view the lives lost as mere statistics, we understand that each life taken carries a rich story.

We, the most imprisoned people in the world, trace the roots of this injustice back to the historical injustices of slavery and settler violence. From that point onward, the perpetuation of slavery and deaths persists. We often say, 'It started with invasion and continues with deaths in custody.' When our people are murdered within the confines of prisons, the institutional state attempts to justify it. The value placed on Black life in Australia is abysmal. We are treated as second-class citizens in our own country.

When we say 'Black Lives Matter' or use the acronym BLM, we are emphasising that these lives matter deeply. We are not minimising or discounting the value of other lives lost. Rather, we are highlighting the fact that Black lives are not being cared for or nurtured in a nation that fails to recognise the worth of Black bodies and souls. We live in a world where vulnerability becomes a target, and punishment is seen as the solution. People readily embrace aspects of Black culture but fail to show up and support Black lives.

Why does this happen?

In 2020, the pandemic forced us all into isolation and loneliness. The digital realm became a platform to witness and confront the undeniable global injustices faced by Black individuals.

The name George Floyd became synonymous with this searing reality. Floyd, an unarmed Black man, was killed by a white Minneapolis police officer. While sitting in a car with two other passengers, Floyd was forcefully removed and handcuffed. Derek Chauvin, the officer responsible, pressed his knee to Floyd's neck for an agonising nine minutes and twenty-nine seconds, despite Floyd's repeated pleas: 'I can't breathe.' It was a moment that shook the world and forced people to confront the harsh reality faced by Black lives, even when COVID-19 was not at the forefront. This moment of isolation due to the pandemic may have provided a glimpse into the ongoing separation and struggle faced by marginalised communities. It revealed how the abuse perpetrated by the state during the pandemic was nothing short of shameful.

Children were denied their rights to familial contact visits, incarcerated individuals were subjected to prolonged periods of isolation, and the rise in deaths and lack of care exposed a national disgrace. At the peak of the COVID-19 crisis in 2020, when lives were already filled with fear, the BLM movement sparked international discourse and action. People took to the streets, recognising that 'Black Lives Matter' was a topic that was finally receiving the attention and importance it deserved.

Mothers who were incarcerated found themselves deprived of visits with their children as a result of COVID-19 restrictions. The pandemic became a tool to deny families the opportunity to reunite, both for those inside correctional facilities and for those outside. This manipulation of COVID-19 protocols had a profound impact, revealing a disturbing aspect of the crisis – its exploitation to prevent essential family connections. It was a truly shameful practice that stripped individuals of their right to see their loved ones during an already challenging time.

Floyd's murder ignited a wave of digital and real-world action, shedding light on the global crisis of policing and the violence enacted by policing systems. I remember organising national protests in Australia on Gadigal country, unsure if people would show up to demand justice for Black lives while balancing the risks of COVID-19. As organisers, we implored everyone to prioritise their safety and provided masks and sanitisers for those who attended. We demonstrated better crisis management than the national leadership at the time. I saw the most at-risk people, my people, elders and aunties lead the change, and hold the fire.

While there was a global virus, another virus was shown: the virus of racism, and its symptoms still continue. As I write this, I remember looking at all the elders and aunties leading. I see their faces, their wrinkles that demonstrate a story or fight they have endured. I am lit with fire and love for these aunties. Each scar, each mark, each wrinkle is a story of the fight they have never given up on. So, I won't give up on them.

The sad reality is that we knew the violence from the police would not stop, even as the pandemic became more manageable. We knew they would continue to hunt to kill us. However, the inspiring number of people who turned up to demand justice for Black lives showed us what we could be as a people and a nation. It was a moment that demanded we strive to do and be better.

Despite efforts by the police to dismiss our fight for justice, they failed because we had the support of the masses. The power of love and strength outweighed the power of hate and racism. While bigots and fascists still remained, our collective power was much stronger.

Lawyers fought in the courtrooms, legal observers supported us on the ground and more than forty thousand people gathered on Gadigal country alone, with similar numbers in surrounding nations and globally.

So, when we say 'Say their name' or 'Black lives matter', we are referring to our united fight and strength in protest.

As a community, we refuse to forget. The truth remains embedded in the land, the water, the sky, and the blood. Our ancestors are always watching.

The impact of COVID-19 left many families subject to removal processes in greater danger. COVID-19 was weaponised to limit visitation between family members and forcibly remove children.

When we talk about reimagining a better world, it may seem out of reach. But we must envision a world where we emphasise transformative justice, care, love and belonging. I dream of a world where we offer support instead of punishment. For example, when we see a struggling family, we should not pathologise or medicalise them. We should simply help, whether it's by buying groceries or by offering our time and support regularly.

Why involve the police? Why report to child protective services? What positive outcome do you expect from removing a child from their family? Seriously, if it's an emergency and you are calling to make a child safety report, or ROSH report, you will be on the phone for hours.

So, seriously, stop and think. Is it an emergency, or can I assist in some way to make this situation better? What are you prepared to do to make what you have identified as a risk or concern less risky? What about a check-in, a simple 'Hey, how are you doing? You right?' or 'I'm heading down the shops. Want a feed? Need anything?'

As a child, all I wanted was for us to be okay. When I was taken away, it broke me in ways I'm not sure can ever be repaired.

When we consider abolitionist care, the process of reimagining and enacting care that goes beyond surveillance, punishment and abandonment of marginalised individuals becomes challenging.

Imagine if, instead of reporting my family and community, people had actually helped us? Imagine if we had adequate healthcare that identified the struggles my father faced and provided him with support? Imagine if my mum wasn't punished by having her children stolen for having an illness that she, in fact, managed so well and was okay despite it.

The family policing system is a business, and it serves as a significant investment for privatisation at the cost of First

Nations lives. It reproduces a cycle of privatisation and wastes funding that could be better used elsewhere.

Did you know that it is far more expensive to keep a child in the family policing system than it is to fund the communities and families themselves? Imagine if we invested in community rehabilitation and support instead.

In 2023, the Productivity Commission found that the cost per child in care varied across jurisdictions, ranging from $61,731 to $150,783 annually. Where data was available, annual costs were higher for residential facilities: between $487,185 and $955,880. This is a shameful expenditure where we are continuing to see no change at all. It's a clear indication of the state's failure to provide alternative care arrangements, and it further reinforces problematic privatisation incentives over the lives of children and young people.

If these funds were provided to community-controlled organisations and families directly, case managers, directors and all these people in high-paying jobs would not have a job. And maybe … just maybe … this is why we continue to see so much harm.

Can you seriously imagine what we could do with our communities if we didn't dedicate funding to the professional kidnappers and industries such as the department?

What if we redirected the funds from family policing and invested them in therapy and psychological support to help heal the trauma experienced by members of our communities due to the colonial system?

Now that you know we invest hundreds of thousands of dollars into the family court system, family policing system and non-government organisations that act as tools of the state to keep children in the child protection system, you can see that these investments are not yielding any significant success. Our children are still being locked up, tortured, abused, and subjected to the most inhumane treatment.

Did you know that the majority of children who are removed today are placed in emergency hotel rooms with only a case worker present?

What if I told you that there are alarm bells ringing around child sexual abuse in statutory out-of-home care? What if I told you that we are causing further harm to children instead of protecting and supporting them?

But what if we could reimagine a better world? A world of liberation, justice and communal care. As a survivor, I believe this is possible.

I often share in my conversations that while we have a serious epidemic of child removal in Australia and globally, specifically against Indigenous, brown and migrant families, we can address it and create whole-of-system change. There are too many children being removed, but not so many that we can't fix this.

As a survivor, I am committed to living on the side of possibility and transformative justice. I must share this message with the world – that we can fight for justice and better care with communal support. Our relationships, our genuine care for each other, are crucial for the wellbeing of our communities and the world. Otherwise, what are we really doing if we don't care about the most targeted and oppressed peoples?

The thing is, once we become aware, we can no longer be unaware. By reading this book, you have taken the time to understand me and the deep struggles my people face.

So, the question is this: what will you do now that you are aware?

The first step is defunding family policing. Defunding the department is a crucial and fundamental step to achieving change. As a people and society, we simply cannot keep funding a violent system that is not generating change for the better but rather inflicting further state violence on the lives of children and families.

Defunding means removing the money that goes into the department and placing those funds directly where it is needed, such as into community support and appropriate public safety programs. It means divesting funds in order to build homes and rehabilitation centres, to provide support for parents and children, and to create transformative places of connection and being.

The family policing system works as another means to criminalise Black children and families. As I've mentioned, when it comes to the privatising of jails and the family policing system, we begin to see the patterns and intersection between children being forcibly removed and their risk of being subject to the criminal justice system.

What I find so deeply sad is that when a child is removed from their family and community and placed into the foster system, in that very moment – though it may or may not be known to the people stealing that child – the raw reality is that they are removing that child and placing that child at severe risk of the prison industry.

To effectively advocate for defunding, it is crucial to analyse the shortcomings and biases of the existing family policing system. By critically examining current policies, practices and power structures, we can lay the groundwork for a more equitable and community-oriented approach. This is a component of abolition and allows for a safer world for Black families and communities.

Defunding the child protection system does not mean abandoning the needs of vulnerable children; rather, it involves reshaping the allocation of resources to better support families within our communities.

The possibilities include reallocating funds towards community-run programs and initiatives that prioritise prevention, early intervention and culturally appropriate support services. By investing in community-led solutions, we can shift the focus from crisis response to holistic and proactive support.

The current child protection system often focuses on crisis response and out-of-home care placements, which can be costly and traumatic for children and families. By defunding this aspect of the system and reallocating funds, greater emphasis can be placed on prevention and early intervention. This can include investing in community-based services that prioritise family preservation, such as parenting programs, in-home support services and mental health resources.

Rather than investing solely in child protection services, reimagining resource allocation involves expanding the focus to encompass broader social determinants of child wellbeing. Investing in initiatives that address poverty, housing insecurity, education, healthcare and other social factors can significantly impact a family's overall stability and reduce the likelihood of child removal.

Community-led initiatives are crucial in supporting First Nations families and communities. In community-run programs, there can be greater ownership and control over the design and implementation of support services. Redirecting funds towards these initiatives can look, for example, like empowering local organisations to provide culturally safe programs that address the specific needs of their community using culturally appropriate methods and practices.

Prevention and early intervention services are also key in addressing the underlying issues that can lead to child removal. By investing in these areas, communities can develop targeted programs that address risk factors, build resilience and support families in crisis. This includes services such as family support workers, family therapy, addiction treatment and trauma-informed care.

Reimagining investment and resource allocation also involves a commitment to tracking and evaluating the effectiveness of these new approaches. By collecting and analysing data specific to community-led programs and prevention strategies, policymakers can gain insights into what works best for First Nations families. This allows for evidence-based decision-making and the adaptation of services to meet evolving needs.

By reimagining investment and resource allocation, we can shift the focus of the child protection system from being reactive to prioritising prevention, early intervention and community empowerment. This approach not only leads to better outcomes for First Nations children and families but also strengthens community capacity, fosters cultural resilience and addresses the root causes of child removal. It works towards non-reformist reforms.

To fully comprehend the child removal crisis faced by First Nations communities, it is crucial to examine the historical context. The child removal crisis facing First Nations children in Australia cannot be understood without acknowledging the profound impact of colonisation and the policies that have systematically disrupted Indigenous families and communities.

The era of the Stolen Generations, spanning from the late 1800s to the 1970s, remains a dark chapter in Australia's history. During this period, Indigenous children were forcibly separated from their families and communities, often based on discriminatory assumptions about their ability to care for their own children. The intent behind these policies was to assimilate Indigenous children into mainstream European culture, severing them from their language, culture and identity.

The consequences of these government-endorsed removals are far-reaching and have been deeply traumatising for generations of Indigenous families. The forced removals created significant barriers to intergenerational knowledge transmission, cultural continuity and community cohesion. The trauma experienced by the Stolen Generations has left a lasting impact on their wellbeing, and social and emotional development.

It is important to recognise that the legacy of the Stolen Generations still affects Indigenous families and communities today. The trauma and loss experienced by previous generations continue to reverberate, amplifying the vulnerability of First Nations children. Historical trauma can manifest in a range of ways, including high rates of mental health issues, substance abuse, suicide and, as mentioned earlier in this long yarn short, targeting by police.

Education is a catalyst for positive change, in particular in tackling the disproportionate rate of removal of First Nations children in Australia. By educating ourselves, promoting cultural safety and fostering collaborative partnerships, we can work towards the interests and rights of children and young people. We can prioritise the rights, wellbeing and self-determination of First Nations children and families.

Only through education can we strive for a future where every child is allowed to grow and thrive within their own community and culture, not be punished by the state.

When I speak of 'consciousness', what I mean is community awareness. How well do you know your community as both an individual and a collective? How well do you trust each other?

Trust is a foundational element in community strengthening and it is essential in shifting away from a reliance on making reports to the child protection system. Trust allows for open and honest communication between families, community members and service providers.

When there is trust, individuals feel comfortable sharing their challenges, seeking advice and accessing support without immediate fear of punitive actions. This open communication fosters a sense of collaboration and partnership, where everyone can work together to address concerns and find solutions.

When families face difficulties or crises, they can turn to their trusted networks for support and guidance. These networks may include family, friends, community leaders, elders and service providers who share a common goal of ensuring the wellbeing of children and families. These relationships provide a safety net and allow for early intervention and assistance before situations escalate.

Within a community, sharing responsibility helps to foster a sense of kinship care for the wellbeing of children. Rather than relying solely on reporting incidents or concerns to the child protection system, community members feel empowered to take collective action to support struggling families. This can involve offering practical assistance, providing emotional support or connecting families with appropriate resources and services.

I see the way the system often responds with punishment or deficits when it comes to identifying issues. I most definitely saw this with my very own family. Therefore, I argue that with education and allowing communities to transform, and adopting strengths-based approaches to addressing child protection concern, we will allow what our ancestors and people dreamed of to be achieved.

Instead of focusing solely on the risks and deficits within families, trust allows for a focus on strengths, resiliency and the positive aspects of individuals and communities. By recognising and building upon these strengths, families are more likely to feel supported and empowered to make positive changes in their lives.

Community allows for the use of restorative practices within the places that make and shape our homes and safe spaces. Rather than relying solely on punitive measures or removals, restorative practices emphasise healing, reconciliation and repairing harm. Trust enables families, community members and service providers to engage in dialogue, understanding and problem-solving to address concerns while preserving the integrity of the family unit.

A trauma-informed approach will support communities. When individuals and families have trust in service providers, they are more likely to feel safe and supported in seeking help for past trauma and healing.

Trust allows for the creation of a safe and non-judgemental environment where trauma can be addressed in a sensitive, empowering and culturally appropriate manner.

Trust is fundamental in building strong relationships and supportive networks within communities. When trust exists with education and awareness, individuals can feel confident in seeking support from their community rather than having to rely solely on reporting incidents to the child protection system.

Trust allows for collaborative problem-solving, strength-based approaches and trauma-informed support, ultimately resulting in stronger families and communities.

Never forget, our communities have utilised these mechanisms for decades; my very own community knew some of our family struggles. In fact, my family was being supported by the community. But the system did not see the community being our go-to as a strength. It bypassed all of this and took it upon itself to decide what was best for my family, me and my future.

Remember there is a better world, one that doesn't have to rely on punishment. I am not naive to problems existing, nor am I naive to understanding we must protect kids at all costs, but protection is not punishment. Punishing families and communities is a world that leads to hate, violence and separation. It's a world that causes deep pain.

WORTHY OF THE
GOOD THINGS

I AM NO STRANGER TO THE existence of problems; I grew up in what many would deem the 'dangerous' parts of our community. I have witnessed the best of humanity and the worst it can offer.

I began this long yarn short with red and blue lights flashing down our street, and these were present more often than the actual streetlights.

I have spent my formative years witnessing horrific events – from heartbreaking suicides and acts of violence to unyielding struggles and inspiring displays of strength.

I have seen what an aunt can do with just $15 to feed an entire family. I have heard wisdom, love and solutions from the minds of both young and old.

When I imagine a better world, I wonder what would the world look like if we provided the opportunities of the privileged to those who may not have been as fortunate? Would we steal away their children? Would we punish them for their poverty? Would we criminalise their battles with addiction?

When I reflect upon what is in the best interests of children, I am constantly faced with a bitter reality: the denial of their genuine desires and voices. The department has an obsession with best interests at the costs of silencing their interests.

Most children simply yearn for the best for their parents, even through their deep struggles. No-one possesses more empathy or understanding than a child and, truthfully, they shouldn't have to bear such burdens.

As adults, it is our responsibility to step in and recognise the support that other adults require. That's on us, not our babies.

In times of pain and harm, I find myself wondering about the origins of these struggles. Are they the result of personal difficulties that the department refuses to recognise? Perhaps these individuals were never offered adequate support. Maybe they have become victims of systemic violence that leads them down a path of poverty.

I cannot help but wonder how much more effective this world could be if only we were to embrace the power of compassion and provide the necessary aid instead of punitive responses.

Often, I look back and envision the alternative life I could have led if my family and community had received the support they deserved. And let me assure you, this is no exaggeration – this support cannot come from the department that takes children from their home, country and place, as they always have historically and presently, playing a role in perpetuating harm.

Our ultimate objective must always be to do no harm whatsoever, to add no more danger. But we know one thing for sure: the welfare system only knows how to add more harm, barriers and obstacles for families and communities.

Make no mistake, my family faced our fair share of difficulties, and we faced them with incredible resilience. However, struggling should never justify the separation of families.

I cherished paydays when my father received his payment, but I despised the bottle shops, Cathy the yandi dealer, TABs and the people who knew Dad's payday and hoped to extract money from him. The arrival of payday meant excitement, as it often meant we would indulge in a take-out meal – a rare treat for us. Joseph and I would fight over the leftovers the next morning, with Pizza Hut being our unanimous favourite.

Sadly, my family never quite grasped the concept of managing finances. Money would come and quickly disappear. There was something about these fleeting moments of joy that we clung to. If I'm being honest, these moments were few and far between, which made us cherish them even more. However, they were short-lived.

Whenever my dad received a small amount from his super fund, he would radiate pure happiness. He was selfless in those moments, and almost every couple of years, he would receive around $3000–$4000. We felt like the richest people in the world, but Dad would generously give the majority of that money to our cousin Peta, who had five children. He had an extraordinary soft spot for her, and her resilience in life was unmatched. Sadly, we had our cracks, but I know that if I were to call Peta, she would be there in a heartbeat. The saddest part is that she always shows up during times of pain, but not during moments of joy – a painful testament to the normality of suffering in our community. However, this shouldn't be regarded as normal. As a community, we are overwhelmed by bad news, grief, deaths and the loss of innocent lives.

The neighbourhood bottle shop saw more of our money than we did. The local betting shops, profiting off the cruel mistreatment of horses, were also prevalent. I despised those establishments.

Yes, we struggled, but it did not have to be this way. As an adult, I reflect and wonder what could have happened if my father had received the support he needed rather than being punished.

What if he had been surrounded by compassion and assistance to heal from the abuse he endured in boys' homes? What if he hadn't faced racism at every turn?

What if my mother had been embraced with love, joy and excitement upon discovering her pregnancy with me? What if she hadn't been pathologised? What if she had been allowed to have what the majority of society takes for granted? What if they hadn't taken away her firstborn son and had instead identified her needs early on?

What if we were provided with housing in an area where we could still avail ourselves of the necessary services without being uprooted to the middle of nowhere?

What if our local community centre was provided with support to meet the needs of the community instead of threadbare funding?

What if we were considered worthy of the good things?

I often hear the narrative that people subject to poverty do not deserve the good things, and I understand how this perception has seeped into the collective consciousness.

I remember being one of the few families at my primary school without a computer. One day, the school principal kindly offered us old computers to take home. Although it meant the world to us and our little family, it also made me realise that we were not deemed worthy of anything new.

But what if we are indeed worthy of the good things?

What if we are worthy of support?

What if we are worthy of being free from racism?

What if we, as individuals and as a community, are truly worthy?

We know our worth, but do you?

There are simply too many children subject to forcible removal. But, equally, there are not so many that we can't fix this, that we can't get it right.

We can create a world, a vision that allows for worthiness and love for all.

What I have learned, both professionally and personally, is that we tend to over-complicate things and lose sight of our initial motivations – especially those in the professional kidnapping field.

I have also come to learn methods and possibilities that can allow for us all to ensure we are focused towards bringing our children home, ending racial violence and protecting the futures of our children and young people.

It is important to refrain from actively engaging or supporting workplaces and industries involved in the forcible removal of children by professional kidnappers. Instead, consider leveraging the valuable skills you have acquired by reflecting on how best to use them.

Take the time to seek guidance from elders, regardless of whether you are Indigenous or not. Engaging with elders in conversation is a profound sign of respect and a valuable opportunity to listen and learn. When you take this step, you are choosing to expand your knowledge and truly embark on ethical practice.

What I often see is when people get to higher positions of authority within the department, they become stale. I mean it: off, gross and too comfortable in their own shoes. They begin to lose sight of the actual goal.

The salary for a senior case manager or director general in the professional kidnapping industry is enough to support four families. What does that tell you?

Here is my little yarn on some ways to combat this.

Refuse participation that makes the professional kidnapping industry stronger. Non-participation is a powerful form of advocacy and raises awareness about issues within the department. It can spark conversations, prompt reflection and encourage others to critically examine their own participation and the patterns they may be involved in.

Non-participation can create space for supporting and promoting alternative systems, initiatives or practices that prioritise ethical values, the safety of our children and keeping families together through addressing issues of poverty and marginalisation.

By redirecting support towards such alternatives, individuals can actively contribute to building a more equitable and just society. It really is the small things we do that add up. When individuals come together to collectively opt out of supporting harmful industries, their combined actions can have a significant impact on driving systemic change.

Implement community-led support networks and resources. Empower local communities to design and deliver culturally responsive support services that meet their specific needs, fostering community ownership and engagement.

Address the intersections and violence of state systems and the risks to children and young people when they are eighteen years of age and about to exit the family policing system. It is crucial to address the risks of sexual exploitation, trafficking and coercion to safeguard them from harm.

Ensure full access to support services, such as housing, financial and education assistance and therapy, for young people who are exiting. The provision of these resources must be non-negotiable. The onus of the long-term safety of children and young people subject to family policing rests on the department – they must ensure every avenue of safety.

Establish culturally competent and diverse care teams. Build diverse care teams that reflect the communities they serve, provide training in cultural competency, and ensure that individuals receive equitable and respectful care regardless of their background. This means greater focus on all intersections and giving decision-making power to the experts in the room (that being the parent, the child and the health or other service provider).

Use trauma-informed care practices and approaches that recognise past traumas, prioritise safety, trust and empowerment in these environments, and support individuals in their healing journey. This means being reflective on where this all begins: colonisation, violence and separation tactics aimed to influence land possession.

Prioritise prevention strategies. Invest in preventative measures such as education, early intervention programs and community outreach to address root causes and reduce the need for reactive responses to crises.

Foster accountability within the department. Establish mechanisms for accountability, and promote transparency, integrity and continuous improvement to address systemic issues promptly, align policies with ethical standards and meet community expectations. Recognise that if the department is unethical, and not practising appropriately, it must be closed down immediately.

Regularly monitor and evaluate care processes to identify areas for improvement, ensure services meet individuals' needs effectively, collect data, listen to feedback, and adapt practices to enhance service quality and impact.

Demand accountability for the historical and current injustices of family policing and the criminal justice system. This means there must be urgent evaluations and audits on the systems that have played crucial roles in murdered, missing and harmed First Nations lives. What we know is history has always had a role in all of this; colonisation is the root from which this violence stems. Urgent inquiries and actioned responses are urgently needed.

Lastly, abolish family policing.

CLOSING

T O MY YOUNGER SELF:

I apologise for not being able to shield you from the pain and challenges that marked our early years together. The impacts of those difficult times are undeniable, but the core of your being, your strength, is unyielding and formidable.

I am deeply sorry that you had to endure the loneliness of those foster facilities and placements, and be tricked into thinking you could never know love or be 'home' – a feeling so unbearable and isolating. But now, I am here for you.

You can shed the weight of that solitude, dear little one, because the adult Vanessa has navigated many obstacles and discovered love in the form of a magnificent Bati warrior from Fiji. She has embarked on journeys in law and social work, dedicating herself to supporting other youth and children, fighting for her people. And, perhaps most importantly, she nurtures her own child in a world where the pain of loneliness has no place. A world where love flourishes, empowering us both to confront life's challenges with unwavering resilience.

I understand that the system was never designed to fully comprehend our needs, and that realisation could have spelled failure for us. But we defied the odds. Not the system, but us. Together, we unearthed truths and forged paths with unwavering determination.

I am full with anticipation for the boundless opportunities that lie ahead, for we are strong, beautiful and rooted in the ancient enduring bloodlines of our ancestors.

I am Bundjalung Widubul-Wiabul.

I am Vanessa, and maybe you found a little of yourself here.

Let us bring our children home.

Together.

To re-imagine is a powerful thing. But I promise you this: you do not have to look far, because our people, my people, are healers, knowledge holders, communicators, solution-driven thinkers and creatives. We have known what works and does not work since the first sunrise.

And I promise you this: we will be here through every sunset and new day that begins.

We will not stop.

We are still here.